Waggoner's Way 1993
has been published in a
Limited Edition
of which this is

Number 838

A list of original
subscribers is printed
at the back of the book.

WAGGONER'S WAY

FRONT COVER: A 'Small' Aveling and Porter, ASC No 47, manufactured in 1906 and bought for £450, is unloaded from the deck of the battleship HMS *Commonwealth* 16,350 tons, in Grand Harbour, Malta, 1913. (Photo: Capt G.C.G. Blunt ASC)

A typical RCT troop in the 1980s: 8 Squadron 27 Regiment RCT, Buller
Barracks, Aldershot.

WAGGONER'S WAY

A century of the Corps' past from
the Journals of the ASC, RASC and RCT
and from Corps photographic archives
1891-1991

EDITED BY
MICHAEL YOUNG

BARON
MCMXCIII

PUBLISHED BY BARON BIRCH
FOR QUOTES LIMITED IN 1993
AND PRODUCED BY KEY COMPOSITION,
SOUTH MIDLANDS LITHOPLATES, HILLMAN PRINTERS (FROME) LTD,
CHENEY & SONS AND WBC BOOKBINDERS

ISBN 0 86023 521 1

CONTENTS

END PAPERS — FRONT: March-past of the RASC on the occasion of King George V's Silver Jubilee Royal Review in Rushmoor Arena, Aldershot, 1935; BACK: caricatures of members of the MT School Officers Producing Centre RASC during the Second World War (1941).

INTRODUCTION

This book marks the end of another chapter in the history of logistic support of the Army, as political and economic changes in the world cause reduction and reorganization throughout the Armed Services. In 1993 the Royal Logistic Corps inherits the tasks and traditions of the Royal Corps of Transport, which evolved from the Royal Army Service Corps, and the Army Service Corps before that, not to mention other predecessors in the 18th and 19th centuries.

Two collections are available to me as the last Editor and Curator of the RCT to illustrate our part in the story: the Journals of the Corps, published continuously since 1891, and the photographic archives of the Corps Museum. The contents of this book are my personal selections from both and it is a matter of some pleasure to be able to display treasures, which hopefully will sparkle in the eye of the beholder.

Whether it is through the medium of words or pictures, the reader can savour the atmosphere at the end of the Victorian era, appreciate snippets from the Boer War, observe early developments in mechanical transport and recognize distinguished work in the First and Second World Wars, not to mention world-wide involvements in keeping the peace at all other times.

Waggoner's Way is not a history book but it does reflect, in good times and bad, something of the everyday experiences of officers and men in the last 100 years. Details appear which would normally be swept away in a broader historical survey, details which in themselves are often unimportant, yet which do offer fascinating glimpses of our past. Some personalities appear who contributed greatly; others flit lightly over the stage. None of them, nor indeed any member of the Corps past or present, should be forgotten, though relatively few names appear; our considerable sporting achievements are minimally reflected here, since sports results make dull reading and most of our sporting photographs only show formal groups, which are less than exciting to all but the cognoscenti. I have tried overall to provide something for everyone.

In turning the pages you might find yourself sharing my sadness and sense of nostalgia for the passing of an era, for an empire on which the sun eventually set and for traditions and a way of life which will never be quite the same again; and yet, at the same time, rejoice with me that a great past can only be a spring-board for a great future, providing the confidence to meet new challenges in a constantly changing world. Looking back is great fun but it is only worthwhile if it provides a source of knowledge and a sense of perspective in looking into the future.

Waggoner's Way is dedicated to all members of the Royal Corps of Transport and its predecessors, to all those who did their best in their own time and to those for whom the memory of things well done is very pleasant.

ABOVE: The first ASC Officers' Mess in Stanhope Lines, Aldershot, demolished c1895. The roof was inhabited by wild cats. BELOW: A course of young officers from a variety of regiments on probation for the ASC c1891. The hut behind them was their accommodation. (A)

THE EARLY YEARS 1891-1914

Aldershot, April 1891. The spirit of improvement seems rife at Aldershot. We noticed in "May's Paper" an advertisement for a shorthand writer, to teach a large A.S.C. class. This is another most useful idea, and would prove of the utmost use to most A.S.C. Clerks. In these days of despatch, the military correspondence system must soon be altered, the tedious long-hand note-taking will be a thing of the past. If officers could dictate their numerous official letters to a shorthand writer, what a saving of time would be affected.

Aldershot. During the greater part of the past month the Camp here has been almost without troops. All the duty soldiers of Infantry regiments and a large number of our Corps have been away at Soberton and East Meon taking part in the Infantry Manoeuvres; it seemed quite odd to walk through the usual busy camp and see whole lines vacant and the dingy huts closed. Both officers and men on the manoeuvres have had a bad time of it owing to the continued wet weather. Everywhere was mud and everything was muddy; our men and horses came in literally covered with mud. Our brethren of the Corps at other stations may congratulate themselves that their company was not called in to take part in the Manoeuvres of this year.

The Theatre was beautifully decorated for the occasion; in fact the decorators would appear to have passed a "course of instruction" in this subject. The stage — draped and covered in flags, and beautiful with flowers, plants and shaded lamps — formed a sort of dais, where those not dancing could sit and watch the brilliant and varied scene beneath, thus reversing the wonted uses of stage and auditorium! There were many charming and picturesque toilettes; and the number of different uniforms added the touch of colour and brightness which always gives the *coup d'oeil* to a military ball.

Practice Dance. The practice dance in connection with the Sergeants' Mess commenced on Wednesday, the 18th November, and a very enjoyable evening's amusement afforded. The kindness of our C.O. in having authorised the Theatre to be used for the purpose adds greatly to the comfort and pleasure of these dances.

Early Morning Coffee. Coffee is now issued free to the rank and file at 5.15 a.m. in the barrack-rooms; the coffee is prepared in the cook-house under the superintendence of Staff Sergt. Shafto, the Master Cook; it is almost needless to say, that this issue to the men before going to morning stables is greatly appreciated by them.

In spite of this most disheartening weather

all worked hard and cheerfully, and we have heard of no hitch in the A.S.C. arrangements under such trying circumstances. A new departure was made this year by Colonel Grattan in the mode of carrying A.S.C.

ABOVE: The Band of the ASC escorts the Sunday Church Parade back to Stanhope Lines in the 1890s. BELOW: A General Service waggon of 12 Company on 'W' Square, c1893. This photograph was later used as a Boer War postcard. (B)

despatches by using cyclists instead or horses, when the nature of the ground permitted it.

Annual Ball, Aldershot, December 1891. The Annual Ball given by the Officers of the Army Service Corps at Aldershot took place on Thursday evening, November 12th, at the A.S.C. Theatre — a building, we may remark *en passant*, pre-eminently suited for such a gathering.

The guests, some three hundred in number, were received by Lieut.-Colonel and Mrs Grattan; and as they arrived with a punctuality worthy of a wider practise, the ball-room was very shortly full, and dancing began with the greatest spirit from the first.

A long programme (in which the valse largely predominated over other dances) was successfully carried through, to the strains of the A.S.C. stringed band, whose performance did great credit to the Conductor — Staff Sergt. Parr.

Cricket, June 1891. The three matches next in order are: A.S.C. v. M.S.C. at the Club House, 25th May; A.S.C. Officers v. Remainder, on on our own Ground, 1st June. Yes, on your own ground. The Commanding Officer, Col. Gratton, having decided that this shall be the opening match on the ground which is to be opened on that date; and if all members of the Corps, past or present, were of the same mind as the writer of these notes, I can honestly assert that nothing short of an earthquake would prevent them from coming to Aldershot to witness the completion of that immense undertaking which has resulted in our possessing, at the present time, one of the prettiest and most compact little cricket grounds that the writer — who has played on a few — has ever had the pleasure to cast eyes upon. It is a work which redounds to the credit of all who have been concerned in its production; from its earliest conception by the Colonel, who has throughout been indefatigable in his supervision of the whole of the details, to the officers who have substantially supported it, and to S.S.M. Rose

who has been the Colonel's willing intelligent agent in all matters affecting it, and down to the youngest soldiers of either branch who has lent a hand towards its completion as representative of his comrades generally. May it long remain a credit to the Corps, and a monument to those whose enterprise, exertion, and liberality we owe its possession.

Cycling Dress, Aldershot, July 1891. With reference to Corps Orders, No. 4 of 10th March, 1890, it is notified for general information that H.R.H. the Commander-in-Chief has been pleased to leave it optional with Commanding Officers to allow soldiers taking cycling exercise to wear dark blue stocking tops.

Sergeants' Mess. The N.C.O's. and Sergts. of the A.S.C. gave a quadrille party in the corps' theatre, on 20th February, which, as usual, was well attended by representatives of every regiment and corps in the garrison. The floor was in splendid condition, and dancing was kept up till an early hour to the strains of the A.S.C. string band, under the conductorship of S.Sgt. Parr, to whom every credit must be given for the state of efficiency to which it has been brought. The president, S.S. Major Rose, carried out his duties very satisfactorily, and a most enjoyable evening was spent.

Corporals' Mess. The annual ball of the corporals, A.S.C., took place in the A.S. Corps Theatre, on the 23rd February 1891, and was largely attended by both military and civilian friends. The string band of the A.S.C. was in attendance, and rendered an excellent programme of dance music. Corporal Fallhan officiated as president, and Corporal Dowling as M.C.

Stanhope Lines Accommodation. The snow-storm, or blizzard, of the 9th March, raged furiously at Aldershot, and the old wooden huts, built immediately after the Crimea, were soon partly embedded. In places where the snow had drifted it was between 3 and 4 feet

ABOVE: Staff of the Transport Office, Aldershot, c1891. They dealt with requests from garrison units for horse transport. BELOW: Stable Lines of 2 Company in Woolwich, 1890s.

deep, and some of the men had to get to work with shovels before they could get out of their quarters.

The wooden huts in the camp are being replaced by brick buildings, but owing to the severe winter not much progress has yet been made with the soldiers' quarters. To reside in wooden huts in the winter is not an unmixed blessing; after a heavy thaw they may be seen at their worst. Desolation and slush outside, inside the wind rushes through every crevice; and as the snow melts, it gradually percolates through the roof.

Conductors of Supplies. The number of conductors of supplies in the army list is rapidly decreasing. Although at the time of the creation of the position but few of the A.S.C. N.C.O's. were fortunate enough to be selected, still as it gives the senior warrant rank in the army to the A.S. Corps, and as it is in many ways a better position than that of Staff-Sergeant Major, it seems a pity that this rank is to die out. Conductors of supplies were the first warrant officers made.

Cycling. This form of recreation has for many years been a popular pastime, and though a few members of the A.S.C. indulge in it, as yet no regular club has been formed in the corps. Apart from the uses of cycling from a military point of view, its votaries may follow it for various reasons; as seekers after health, sightseers, would-be reducers of corpulence, or perhaps as economical travellers.

A cycling club need not be limited to members of the A.S.C. at Aldershot, but could include every home station, and might serve to keep up many a friendship that otherwise might die out. For instance, one wheelman is ordered to Portsmouth from Aldershot; a pass and a couple of hours will take him to Petersfield, when he can meet an old pal from Aldershot. And who would not prefer the grip of a friendly hand (for auld lang syne) and half-an-hours's chat over old times to half-a-dozen letters? Besides which, letter writing is said to be a lost art. In this matter a closer

connection might be established between all stations, say, within 80 miles of each other, than has hitherto existed. However, I must leave the formation of a club to some energetic cyclist, hoping to hear from one soon.

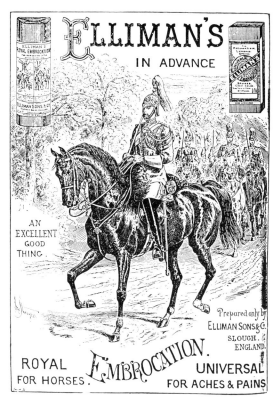

Letter To the Editor A.S.C. Gazette. In the Royal Engineers' lines, Aldershot, there is a very good barber's shop, nicely kept and fitted up. It is much appreciated by all ranks, and found to be a great convenience. Would it not be possible to start an A.S.C. shop at this station? I would suggest that there be two rooms, one for Officers and one for W.O., N.C.O., and men.

I am, Sir, yours truly,
SHAVER
Aldershot,
March 3rd, 1891.
(Accommodation cannot be found — Editor.)

Trumpets, May 1892. Authority having been received for the issue of trumpets in lieu of

ABOVE: A group of officers (Major, Lieutenant and two Second Lieutenants) pose with dog, Chatham, 1893. BELOW: A convoy rests on the march, c1897.

bugles, our "Trumpeters" are rapidly mastering the "calls" on the former instruments.

Our useful little "String Band" made a new departure on Easter Sunday evening by playing the music for a Choral Service in the "Iron Church" in the presence of quite an unusually large and distinguished congregation.

Volunteers, August 1892. Most of the Volunteer Infantry Brigades have now an organized Supply Detachment for carrying on the Brigade Supply duties. Our uniform is being adopted by them trimmed with silvered lace and buttons. We cannot say if this is universal, but see one brigade is adopting it, and very neat it looks.

Home District. (Godalming) July 1892. No 6 and 16 Co's A.S.C. from Chelsea were billetted at Godalming on Thursday, the 12th May, en route to Dublin. On the arrival of the Co's at Godalming the Vicar, the Rev. Mr Burrows, invited the officers, NCO's and men to tea and afterwards a smoking concert.

The Vicar to ensure that each man was informed of the entertainment issued about 100 written invitations, and sent a curate around the billets to distribute the invitations to each man.

All the officers and almost all the NCO's and men attended the entertainment in the evening, when a substantial tea was provided and served to the men by Mrs Burrows and other ladies. After tea the officers arrived and a smoking concert commenced.

After the entertainment had commenced, the Vicar hearing that some of the men had not come, took a Sergt with him around the public-houses, and by persuasion got those to come that were first inclined to spend the evening elsewhere.

Natal and Zululand, December 1892. Major F. A. Le Poer Trench has assumed command of the A.S.C. in Zululand, and by the many newspaper accounts he is the means of

enabling the men under his command to enjoy a good deal of recreation, cricketing, etc.

Staff Sergt. Major Hennessy, Sergt Sabine, Corpl. Springett,, Milton and Toogood are stationed in Zululand; Corpls. Springett and Milton being in charge of the Field Bakery, where they provide daily for the wants of the Zululand garrison.

The Transport establishment with its head quarters at Eshowe is under command of Major Trench with civil conductors — Murchison, Le Brun, Tavenon, Dean and Gadwin as his working staff.

Conductor Le Brun, with 12 wagons and 120 mules recently arrived at Pietermaritzburg from Zululand on convoy, and whilst at Pietermaritzburg, was in charge of Transport arrangements in connection with the annual camp of the Natal garrison. He returned to Zululand with the convoy loaded with supplies.

Football, Aldershot. We are pleased to notice a marked improvement in our Football Team at this station this season; they play considerably better than the team has done for the past three years. Capt. Longden and Lieut. Kaye have joined them; they are two excellent additions, and we may now look for a continued improvement, until the Corps is able to compete in the Army Cup Matches; some of our readers may think us too ambitious in this line, but in a large Corps like ours there should be little difficulty in getting, training, and keeping together a team able to hold its own against a number of Clubs which now compete.

Our present team plays very pluckily; but may we say, in a spirit of friendly critcism, requires more practice generally, especially in passing. Could not two or three practices a week be managed, or a few Inter-regimental matches be arranged to acquire a better knowledge of one another's play? In our match against the Royal Warwick Regiment this was very noticeable, for it was neither greater weight nor speed which enabled that Regiment to defeat the A.S.C., but simply

ABOVE: Boer War 1899 - 1902: waggon teams and a variety of ASC men, civilian drivers and conductors, and BELOW: waggons take care crossing a spruit.

their combination — that is their playing to one another was superior to ours.

Egypt-Cairo, February 1893. Our Christmas was a merry one, and was well and wisely spent. The room, which was decorated for the occasion, reflected great credit on the N.C.O.'s and men (Corpls. Coffey, Titterrell and Whiffer, and Ptes. Batt and Moss) who were chiefly responsible for the elaborate adornment of the walls, ceiling and windows, and the beautifully worked mottoes (wishing officers and families all sorts of good things and blessings), a work which required a good deal of taste, skill and labour in a place where nice holly and berries are not to be had.

Corps and Station News, March 1893. The following Retired Officers (late A.S.C.) have been temporarily employed under Art. 429 of the Royal Warrant of 25th. May, 1892, viz.:- Major E. J. Dolton, Qr. Mr.; Capt. T Baillie, Qr. Mr., at Portsmouth, from 1.2.93 vice Major J.C. Gore, Af. Comt.; Capt E. Phillips, Qr., at Brighton, from 7.2.93., vice Bt. Major J. A. W. Falls.

Staff Clerks. The Royal Warrant of 24.11.92 (published by Army Order 1 of 1893) having provided for the formation of a Staff Clerk Section of the Corps, the administration of the existing, and future, body of Staff Clerks has been vested in the A.Q.M.G., A.S.C.

Postings, May 1893. Major F. T. Clayton reported his arrival from China on 24th March, and has relieved Capt. F. W. Steele of the command of 2 Co. Capt. Steele embarked for Sierra Leone on 22nd April in relief of Capt. F. W. B. Koe, who will shortly complete a tour of service on the West Coast of Africa.

The Regimental Dinner, July 1893. The Officers' Regimental Dinner is now, we are glad to record, an annual institution with an annually increasing attendance. In a scattered Corps like ours occasions that give opportunity of meeting brother officers, of renewing old acquaintanceships, and forming new ones are few and far between, so that our annual gathering is the more available. As it becomes more generally realised that "Derby Day" is also "Dinner Day" we hope that more of the officers who have left us may be able to look ahead, and arrange to join us once a year for a talk over old times. Some few have already joined the dinner club and we hope more will follow. The dinner club was only

ARMY SERVICE CORPS.

formed at the end of last year and its benefits will be more felt as time goes on, at first starting and before a fund is really formed. The payment for the dinner cannot be much reduced, but it is hoped that in the early future it may be possible not only to make the dinner cheaper to members, but also to reduce the amount of subscription from officers abroad.

The dinner of 1893 was held as usual at the Metropole, and was attended by seventy-nine

ABOVE: Boer War: 'Hotel' accommodation provides some protection from Boer artillery, Kimberley, (C) and BELOW: the ASC Officers' Mess kitchen and cooks, Stellenbosch, 1899.

officers, General Sir R. Biddulph, G.C.M.G., C.B., Quarter-Master General kindly consenting to preside.

We cannot help thinking that many of the seventy-nine must have been agreeably surprised at the excellence of the string band, nineteen members of which attended from Aldershot, and give unmistakable evidence of their skill. It is so easy to have a poor band, and so exceedingly difficult to make a good one that all praise is due to the Band Committee, to Trumpet Major Parr and to those who work so hard and so cheerfully under him, for securing so complete a success.

It was very noticeable this year that so many officers were able to come from distant stations, from Ireland, from Devonport, from the North of England; and had not sudden duties interfered at the last minute the number of dining would have been even larger than they were.

Army Temperance Association, Aldershot. The first monthly meeting of the A.S.C. branch of the A.T.A. was held on Monday night, the 19th June, in the Theatre. There was a very large attendance including Col. and Mrs. Bridge and nearly all the officers and ladies of the Corps who helped to make the programme very entertaining.

Since the formation of the Branch nearly 200 pledges have been taken, so the society may be said to have made a very respectable start in the A.S.C. here.

A.S.C. Horticultural Show, August 1893. On Monday, 17th ult. the annual horticultural and floral show of the Army Service Corps was held in the theatre of the Corps. This year the show was held much earlier than last, and the exhibits were very good all round. There was however but little choice as to time, owing to the pending hard work of the manoeuvres. The exhibits, numering about 300 or so were beautifully laid out on one long six feet wide table running the whole length of the theatre, and on other tables at the sides of the theatre. These tables had also been charmingly decorated with flowering shrubs, plants, grasses, &c., kindly supplied from the extensive nursery gardens of Mr. Rattray, of Ash Vale.

ASC Band. It will be interesting to our readers to learn that the necessary permission has been obtained for the A.S.C. voluntary dismounted marching band, consisting of 21 performers, to play on the following occasions:- (1) On church parades; (2) on the authorised holidays, as fixed by Art. 793, Royal Warrant, at any time during the day; (3) on any week-day after 4 p.m., excepting Saturday when it may play after 1 p.m.; (4) at funerals of their comrades. That if played at other hours, the members of it should lose their corps pay (which would be made up to them from the Officers' Band Fund). A further detailed account will be given in our next. The string band will be maintained as hithertofore for indoor purposes.

Regimental Registers for Civil Employment. All Officers of the Corps are requested to use their earnest endeavour to find employment for Reserve and Discharged Soldiers of the Corps; and it is suggested that if there is no local objection, a notice in bold print, in some such terms as below, should be fixed outside the barrack gate at stations where these Registers are directed to be kept.

Civil Employment. A Register of names of Reserve or Discharged Soldiers of good character, who are thoroughly qualified as

Clerks	Butchers	Harness Makers
Grooms	Carpenters	Caretakers
Bakers	Smiths	&c. &c. &c.

is kept by the Officer Commanding A.S.C. in these Barracks.

Employers are Invited to Apply

Aldershot Barracks. Those whose lot it is to visit this station after an absence of some little time, cannot fail to be impressed with the rapid rate at which building improvements are progressed with, and soon the Camp will be unrecognisable by those who knew it only

ABOVE: Boer War: Lieut H. S. Buckle ASC (father of Major-General D.
H. V. Buckle) and clerks of the Supply Depôt, Springfontein, Orange
River Colony, July 1900. BELOW: 26 Company ASC, Aldershot, 1903,
after their return from South Africa in September 1902.

as it was. The huts are fast disappearing, "lines" after "lines" are rapidly handed over to the demolishers; from our position in Camp, our quondam dwellings were the last attached. The men's huts in "S" lines are down, and most of those in "R" lines are no more, having been destroyed to clear the site for the new married quarters for R.E. and A.S.C., and for two rows of Warrant Officers quarters. The Sergeants' Mess is now temporarily located in "I" block until a building is erected. The Officers' Mess will be situated under Thorn Hill, facing the A.S.C. Recreation Ground and the road to the Supply Depot.

A.S.C. Band. Volunteers to fill up the vacancies through men transferred to reserve, those discharged, going abroad, or promoted, &c., are asked for. Such applicants must have a certain knowledge of, and able to read music. Clarionet and oboe players are specially needed.

It is computed that the maintenance of the Band yearly, will be £150. The entire expense is born by the officers. The whole of the instruments belong to the Officers' Amusement Fund, except four violins and one cornet, the performers of which play on their own instruments.

The debt of the Band Fund at present is about £70. It is hoped it will show a credit next spring. About £50 a year is subscribed by Officers at out-stations.

J. HORNIBLOW, Capt. (Band President).

Manoeuvres, October 1893. The 1st of September, found nearly the whole of the Aldershot Detachment of the Corps distributed at the various Rest and Manoeuvre Camps, busy from morning to night at their multitudinous duties, and in spite of the novelty of their surroundings and the various companies being split up for duty with Divisions and Brigades, the work progressed with machine-like regularity, every change of plan being flashed by the telegraph for the information of all concerned, from Ashbury, the Head Quarters of the A.S.C.

Woolwich, November 1893. The annual inspection by the A.Q.M.G., A.S.C., took place on the 23rd October. The mounted marching order parade was formed up on Plumstead Common at 9.30 a.m., and within a few minutes of that time the inspecting officer, accompanied by Major Bunbury, D.A.Q.M.G., arrived on the ground. After minutely inspecting the eight companies, the A.Q.M.G. proceeded to the saluting base, and the companies ranked past. The thick mud, caused by the incessant heavy rain of the previous day, rendered any other movements almost impossible. On return to barracks the regimental books, institutions, stables and barrack rooms were inspected. After lunch the usual cloak and cape parade took place, and the inspection concluded with company offices and books. The A.Q.M.G, and D.A.Q.M.G. dined with the officers in the evening. In a morning order on the 24th, the Commanding Officer conveyed to all ranks the pleasure afforded to the A.Q.M.G. at all he had seen, especially when the weather and the time of year were taken into consideration. All the wagons having been out in the open in the drenching rain and fog on Sunday, the burnished steel work was spoilt, especially by the fog, which got in everywhere.

Vanishing Aldershot and Aldershot Redivivus – 1854-1894. December 1893. Those of us who knew Aldershot only in the days of wooden huts, will soon find it difficult to fix landmarks by which to guide their dimmed recollections. The demolition of the old wooden huts goes on apace, and old familiar buildings, in which so many past generations

ABOVE: The first internal combustion engined vehicle of the ASC, a 'Stirling', made in Edinburgh 1903, was called the 'spit and cough machine'. BELOW: Fowler Lion steam engine of 77 Company in the Curragh, Ireland, in 1904. Coal was carried in the first trailer and freight in the remainder.

of soldiers lived and in which so many generations of present and future soldiers and citizens first saw the light, have already fed the flames of many a Volunteer or Manoeuvre camp fire.

The single men of the Corps are already housed in the new red-brick two-storey blocks, of which there are nine, each with a construction for 110 men. The change from the old drafty hut barrack-rooms to dry well-built permanent brick buildings is thoroughly appreciated by the men. The site occupied by the new buildings is that of the old Parade Ground, where in the past an endless flow of recruit officers and men have followed the serpentine intricacies of "movements by fours," and struggled with the unaccustomed carbine.

It will not be long before the building of villa-like semi-detached red-brick quarters for the Quarter Masters and Riding Master will be actually begun. Quarters for Warrant Officers and married soldiers are also to be constructed on a scale which for comfort and convenience will be a distinct departure in military domestic architecture.

The Canteen, Sergeants' Mess, Recreation Room, shops, offices and schoolrooms are to soon appear on plans calculated to meet the modern development of these institutions. For the men, ball-courts, baths, skittle alleys, etc., will be built in convenient proximity to the lines.

Nor will the Army Service Corps School of Instruction be forgotten in the erection of two good-sized lecture rooms, with a museum or model room between.

Facing west, and overlooking the green sward of the Corps Recreation Ground slowly rises from its foundations a large pile, which will eventually contain the Officers' Mess and Officers' Quarters. The Mess Establishment will be in the middle, and flanking it on either side 18 officers' quarters, the latter on two floors. Over the centre entrance porch, leading to the mess premises, will be the Army Service Corps arms, now familiar to all of us on our note paper, and the tessellated

flooring of the hall will be embellished by A.S.C. in monogram. The messroom will be 40ft. in length and 22ft. 6in. in breadth, with a corresponding pitch of ceiling. Quarters for the Mess Sergeant, waiters' room, silver room, store room, cellarage and other requirements, have not been forgotten in the plans. The queer old ramshackle, but not uncomfortable, mess-hut will soon be little more than a memory — and a photograph!

Aldershot then seems to bid fair to become a head quarter station worthy of the Corps at large, one in the well being and well doing of which all other stations of the Corps may take an interest and a pride. The large number of officers and men stationed there (nearly 1,200 at this moment,) the magnitude of its establishments all point to it as a place of increasing importance in the future. As the Royal Artillery have Woolwich, the Royal Engineers Chatham, so have the Army Service Corps a Mecca to which all Army Service Corps members Make one pilgrimage at least, (if not indeed many), before their official existence is extinguished by Royal Warrant.

"FLOREAT, ALDERSHOT."

Water Transport, August 1894. The question generally of Transport by water is exciting such universal attention at the present time, and is likely to be of such extreme importance in the future, more especially in the event of war, that a brief outline of the duties connected with the subject may prove not less uninteresting to the Army Service Corps.

The department is organised under the Q.M.G. to whom the D.A.A.G. Transport is directly responsible for the administration and for the general working of the executive duties for the conveyance of stores between Woolwich Arsenal and other stations. The fleet of W. D. vessels is divided as follows:- Sea-going steamers, steam launches, steam barges, sloops, sailing barges, boats and pontoons in addition to a heavy gun barge at Woolwich, amounting to a total aggregate of 119 at home and 127 abroad.

ABOVE: Cpl Symonds with his new 'mount', Aldershot c1903. (D)
BELOW: The light car establishment in London, 1904; left to right: 8 hp
Wolseley, 10 hp Lanchester, 8 hp Wolseley and 15 hp Siddeley.

The respective ranks of the crews of these vehicles are:- Masters, mates, boatswains; 1st engineers, 2nd engineers, engine drivers; leading stokers, stokers, A. B. seamen, ordinary seamen and boys, who are paid at the various rates for their grades fixed per calendar month.

The crews wear a regulation uniform, which need not be described here, and which they can provide and keep at their own expense, or obtain from Pimlico on repayment. The engineers and stokers are supplied with two canvas suits of working clothing yearly free of cost, issued from Pimlico and accounted for by D.A.A.G. Transport, to whom demands for all stations are forwarded.

Officers' Mess, Aldershot, February 1895. On the 26th January the Officers' Mess Establishment here was transferred from the old hut to the New Mess, the formal house-warming taking place on Wednesday, 30th January, when a Dinner was given in the New Mess Room, to which Lt. Col. Bridge and the Officers at Aldershot invited representatives of the Corps from all stations in the United Kingdom.

The Band played the following Selection: Programme.- 1, March, "Tommy's Own," Crook; 2, Overture, "Le Diademe," Hirman; 3. Valse, "Little Christopher Columbus," Coote; 4, Intermezzo, "Song D'amour apres le Bal," Czibulka; 5, Selection, "Iolanthe," Sullivan; 6, Valse, "Go Bang," Kiefert. "God Save the Queen." Extras. — Intermezzo, "Harlequinade," Forster; Danse Espagnole, "Espana," Brandts; Valse, "Douglas Gordon," Metzler. Conductor, Staff Sergt. Bryce.

Postings, March 1895. Captain Hamnett, who is at the top of the roster for foreign service, wishes to exchange. Address c/o Sir C. R. McGregor, Bart., & Co., 25, Charles Street.

1st Cl. Staff Sergt. Major Higgins, who is on the top of the Foreign Service Roster would be glad to hear from any Warrant Officer anxious to go abroad; with a view to an exchange.

Canes. Regimental Canes mounted with the corps crest, white metal mounts, 1/3, silver mounts 5/-; Silver Crest Brooches in lush cases 4/6; Whips with corps crest, white metal mounts and leather handles from 2/3, may be had from Staff Armourer, R. Y. Muir, A.S.C., South Camp, Aldershot.

N.B. — All kinds of whip and cane mounts kept in stock, orders by post promptly executed.

THE ARMY SERVICE CORPS
"ALLY SLOPER'S CAVALRY"
"ARMY SLAVEY CORPS"

Cycling, South Eastern District, October 1895. The Bicycle Club is growing in popularity and now numbers 60 members. Practice is indulged in every evening.

Company Outing, No. 29 Co., Transport and Supply, had an outing on 3rd Sept., granted by the Commanding Officer, Major J. C. Oughterson. They entrained at Shorncliffe station at 12-30 p.m. and proceeded to to Deal,

ABOVE: Dining room, Woolwich Officers' Mess, c1903, complete with wild boar heads, weapons and other trophies. BELOW: The ASC football team of 1904-05: three players are wearing AFA badges and two the Aldershot Command badge, goalkeeper sports medallions.

the place arranged for the outing, arriving there about 1-30 p.m., and proceeded to the Clarendon Hotel, which is situated close to the sea, where dinner was laid out on a grand scale, and, needless, to say, ample justice was done to the same. After dinner, Co. Sergt. Major Harlow proposed the health of H.M. the Queen and the Royal Family; and after an interval, the health of our Commanding Officer and Lieut. F. M. Wilson was proposed, not forgetting Lieut. H. G. Garsia, who was on sick leave. The Company dispersed about 3 p.m. to take pleasure in the open; some went boating, others indulged in billiards, Donkey riding, etc., whilst others went sightseeing. All hands returned to the Hotel at 6 p.m. where a splendid tea was provided and enjoyed by all.

Barber. A Barber's Establishment has been opened in connection with the corps at this station. Two rooms have been comfortably fitted up, and all the necessary appliances for hair-dressing, shampooing, (hot and cold water) and shaving provided. Show cases are on view, and a number of useful articles are on sale at very moderate rates. The head barber is a reserve man, and he receives a weekly wage. He has assistants from men of the corps, who attend during their off time. The stoppage for the rank and file will remain as theretofore, viz. 1d. per month. The W.O.'s, Staff Sergts. and Sergts. (for whom a separate room is provided) pay 2d. for each hair cutting. The charge for shaving will be 1d. for all ranks, and for shampooing, 1½d. It is confidently expected that this shop will become so well established that in a very short time it will be possible to altogether do away with the stoppages for the rank and file, and the work then performed paid for at a moderate charge.

Opening of the New Sergeants' Mess, Aldershot, November 1895. The new Sergeants' Mess was formally opened on 4th October. It stands on the site of the old Commanding Officer's quarters at the corner of "R" Lines, and is a handsome building. The main entrance opens into a spacious dining room, the billiard and reading rooms being at each end of the building and having separate entrances. There is also a capacious bar, and caterer's quarters, supper rooms, ablution room, yard, etc. Mr. Jones, North Camp, is carrying out the furnishing arrangements, and when completed it will be one of the most comfortable messes in camp.

The opening celebration took the form of a vocal and instrumental concert. A large number of invitations were issued, and nearly every Corps in garrison was represented amongst a brilliant assemblage, which packed the room in every part. The tables were prettily decorated with flowers and ferns, the A.S.C. Station Football Cup, and other silver trophies, lending additional attraction to the general appearance. The Corps band was present and performed several choice selections.

The lion of the evening was undoubtedly Master Ricardo, a promising young comedian only 13 years of age, whose songs in character raised much merriment. He commenced by expounding the virtues of "Beer, beer, glorious beer," and judging by the hearty manner in which the chorus was sung, the audience perfectly agreed with his views; he next told of the strange adventures of "Miss Clementina Brown," and also of another young lady who it appears "was in his class"; he concluded a most humorous repertoire with a little ballad entitled "For the sake of the little ones at home," in which the comic element was again conspicuous. Young Ricardo proved himself an artiste of no mean ability, and should make a name amongst comedians of the future. We wish him every success. Bk. Col. Sergt. Bradley, as usual, was quite at home with the banjo, his sentimental ditty about "A little grog blossom that grew on his nose," being excellently rendered. Sergt. Wildman recited "The midnight charge" most effectively.

London. The A.S.C. detachments at this station left for Ashanti as follows:- The first portion, under Capt. C. W. King, left on the

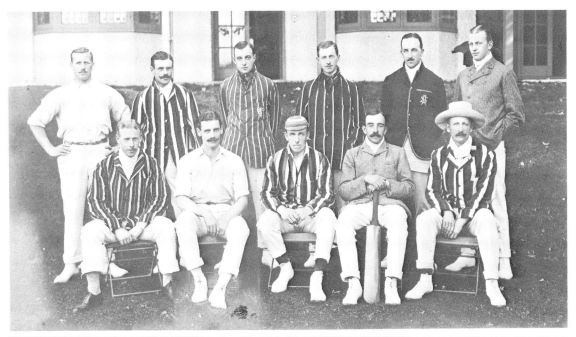

ABOVE: The ASC cricket team of 1907: Lieut E.H. Fitzherbert, later Inspector R.A.S.C. in WW2, is fourth from the left, standing. BELOW: Irish Command Manoeuvres in 1907; ASC vehicles in Ballinakill.

15th ult., the second with Lieut. Col. Ward, on the 22nd. They each left by the midnight train from Euston to Liverpool for embarkation. The first detachment went from Euston with many expressions of "God speed" from their comrades. The departure of the second detachment, with Sir Francis Scott, commanding the Expedition, was the occasion of a general turn-out, who "hurrahed" with truly A.S.C. vigour. The departure of the second detachment was witnessed by Major Gen. Lord Methuen, C.B., C.M.G., commanding Home District, Colonel Mackinnon, A.A.G., Capt. Dawson O.C. A.S.C., Lieut. Glen, A.S.C., and a large gathering of the general public — especially ladies — who were very enthusiastic, the ladies making a patriotic display of handkerchiefs. May our comrades return from Africa as well and hearty as when they left London.

Opening of the New Library, February 1896. It may be of interest to our readers, especially those who have been in Aldershot, and to those who will shortly be coming here, to know that the new building, consisting of a Reading Room, Recreation (billiards, etc.) Room, Coffee Shop, Dining Room, Grocery Bar, Drapery Establishment, Fish and Vegetable Shop, Office, and Steward's and Librarian's quarters has been opened, and is now in full swing. A view can be had from the recreation room of the football and cricket matches that take place on the Corps recreation ground. The billiard and games room is about the largest in the camp, being about 100 feet long and 40 wide. The coffee stall and dining room is admirably fitted up, and something substantially cooked may be obtained for supper, as well as a cup of tea, cocoa, or coffee in the early morning, and I daresay other viands at mid-day. The grocery (dry canteen), drapery establishment, and vegetable store, need not be described, except as being large and most suitable for the purpose. Mr. Chamberlain has the control of the grocery establishment, and Mrs.

Chamberlain manages the drapery, etc. The duties of librarian have been given to Pte. Davies. The old huts where these establishments were formerly are about to be demolished, to make room for other new buildings. These new buildings are a great boon to the men, as they are one of the many items of which the comforts and enjoyments of a soldiers' life is made up. We are sure they will be very much appreciated.

My word if I catch you — !

Drivers, April 1896. The Privates and Drivers held their annual ball in the Theatre, on 25th ult. There was a numerous gathering, including the Commanding Officer and Mrs. Bridge, and several officers of the Corps. The music was supplied by the A.S.C. band, and dancing was indulged in till 2 a.m. The supper tables were laid out in a splendid manner, and full justice was done to the many tempting viands. The floral decorations were all that could be desired, and the general appearance of the theatre was the subject of much favourable comment.

Ashanti, Aldershot, June 1896. An Ashanti war drum and silver stool have been presented to the Officers' Mess by the undermentioned officers of the Corps who took part in the recent expedition to Ashanti:- Lieut. Col. Ward, C.B., D.A.A.G., Lieut. Col. Clayton, Major Donovan, Capts, King, Bernard, Mathew, Thornton, Thring, and Hall, Lieuts. Wilson, Armstrong, Atkins, and Archerley, Lieut. & Qr. Mr.'s Edwards and Challoner. The war drum, which has been mounted on a pedestal, now ornaments the

ABOVE: The first ASC caterpillar on trial in 1907. The 13 ton Hornsby
won the 1st prize of £1000 in 1904 but proved too slow and cumbersome
for the Army. BELOW: ASC and hired Pickford steam engines (Aveling
and Porter and Fowler) with the Repair Train on manoeuvres.

main entrance, while a suitable position is being prepared for the stool. These trophies will prove interesting relics of an expedition in which the Corps played so prominent a part.

Cycling, - Aldershot, August 1896. H.R.H. The Duke of Connaught inspected the military cyclists in his command on 24th July, on the Queen's Parade. The A.S.C. contingent consisted of nine Officers and 29 W.O.'s N.C.O.'s and Men. After the inspection the whole party went for a run, the Duke of Connaught and his Staff heading the procession.

Aldershot Inspection. The Annual Inspection of the Corps at this station took place on Thursday, 13th ult. The G.O.C. Cavalry Brigade was deputed to make this inspection on behalf of H.R.H. The Duke of Connaught, G.O.C., Aldershot District. The parade was formed up on the Sands, in Home Service Marching Order, at 9.30 a.m. After the mounted parade a visit was made to the Riding School, where an Officers', W.O.'s, N.C.O.'s and Recruits' ride took place. The stables, barracks, and Officers' Mess were next visited. After dinner the Regimental and Company Books were examined, and complaints disposed of. The School of Instruction, Canteen, Library, and Workshops were next visited, after which the cast horses were inspected, and a visit to the Regimental Schools brought the inspection to a close. The result of the inspection was that the G.O.C. Cavalry Brigade requested that his entire satisfaction (especially with reference to the excellent turn out of the mounted parade, and the smooth working of all branches of the Corps) may be communicated to all concerned. The Commanding Officer (Lieut. Col. H. N. Bunbury) also congratulated all ranks upon the result, which was only obtained by the hearty co-operation of the entire detachment.

Letter to the Editor, June 1898
Dear Sir, Knowing that there are a great many Freemasons in the Corps, it has occurred to me that a Corps Lodge could be easily founded, and be acceptable to the Officers, Warrant Officers, and Non-Commissioned Officers, members of the Craft. I am convinced, as an old Mason, that such would tend to bring all together in a friendly and Masonic spirit. I should be very pleased to assist in this object, and as you have kindly offered to act as secretary, opinions on the proposal could be either addressed to you or myself.

Believe me,
Yours faithfully
Geo. J. PARKYN, Lieut.-Colonel (R.L.).

Postings, February 1899. Captain S. L. Reynolds, Maryhill Barracks, Glasgow, would be glad to arrange an exchange with any Captain stationed in England.

Field Glasses & Whistles. Corps Order 39; February. It is notified for general information that Field Glasses and Whistles will in future be worn and carried by Officers of the Corps, as directed in paragraph 1971, Queen's Regulations. The Whistle will be of the same pattern as used by the Metropolitan Police, and will be attached to a silk lanyard, the colour of the frock. Field Glasses will be carried in a brown leather case when attached to the saddle.

Distinguished Conduct Medal. Sergeant George Gordon, 3 Co., A.S.C., was presented with the Medal for Distinguished Conduct in the Field, by Her Majesty the Queen at Windsor Castle on 11th May. The act for which the coveted decoration was awarded is thus briefly described:- During the disturbance in Crete last year, the Rebels, at about 3 p.m., on 6th Sept., opened fire on the Greek Hospital; there were about 30 patients in Hospital at the time, besides a small British Garrison, consisting of detachments of the Highland L. Infantry, A.S.C., and R.A.M.C., and about 30 Maltese Drivers. — Pte. McNeill, H.L.I., who was employed as a signaller, and was on duty about 50 yards away from the Hospital, received a severe bullet wound in

Barrack room comfort in 1908, Aldershot: the Wheeler Corporal demonstrates the use of the standard issue folding bed, while Cpl Harry Perkins (rear) looks on.

the side, and immediately fell. Sergt. Gordon, who carried the Union Jack in front of the rescue party, went to his assistance, with Lieut. Clark and six men of the H.L.I., and the stretcher party of the R.A.M.C., and under a heavy cross fire, brought the wounded man into a place of safety, but not before he had again been wounded, the rebels at this time being at close quarters. During the melee Ptes. Weston and Allison, H.L.I., were killed, and Lieut. Clark and Pte. Biddiscombe, R.A.M.C., were wounded. Pte. McNeill, who had been so courageously rescued, succumbed to his injuries on the following morning. The Union Jack which was carried by Sergt. Gordon was riddled with bullets, but, by a miraculous intervention of Providence, the bearer of the flag escaped unhurt. — Sergt. Gordon arrived at Windsor Castle about 2 p.m. on 11th of May, and was met by a Court official, and, after luncheon in the Castle, proceeded to the Main Corridor of the State apartments. At 3.30 p.m. Her Majesty the Queen entered the State reception room, and all who were to be decorated were conducted to her presence, the Queen personally affixing the decoration to the breast of each recipient.

Aldershot, Review. Her Majesty the Queen held a review of about 15,000 troops, on Laffan's Plain, on 26th ulto. The Queen was accompanied by H.R.H. the Prince of Wales, H.R.H. the Duke of York, H.R.H. the Duke of Connaught, H.R.H. the Duke of Cambridge, H.R.H. the Grand Duke Michael of Russia, H.R.H. Princess Christian, H.R.H. the Duchess of Connaught, H.R.H. Princess Victoria of Schleswig-Holstein, and H.R.H. Princess Clementine of Belgium. The Corps was represented by No. 1 Co., under the command of Capt. A. E. Longden. After the royal salute was given the troops marched past, then the Infantry returned in Brigade lines of quarter columns, after which the Cavalry and Artillery galloped past; the proceedings terminated with an advance in line towards the Royal enclosure, the Royal salute was given, and the massed bands

played "God Save the Queen". There was a tremendous crowd of spectators, and the afternoon being fine, the scene was most brilliant.

"WEST COAST."

South Africa, October 1899. Great excitement was caused in this station (Aldershot) upon receipt of orders holding the following Companies in readiness for service in South Africa at an early date, viz.:- Nos. 13, 14, 16, 20, 21, 24, 26, 30, 40, and details of 18 and 38 Cos. Thoughts of everything save service abroad were thrown aside, and the final preparations were commenced; parties were sent under the command of C.S.M. Sadler and C.S.M. Way to Hounslow and West Croydon respectively, to draw equipment, which was drawn, packed, and forwarded to Aldershot without a hitch. The equipment of No. 40 Coy. was placed on board at Southampton, the companies embarking on the 6th October in the *Braemar Castle*, under the command of Lieut. Colonel Clayton, A.S.C.

Curragh. Much excitement was caused in camp on the evening of the 9th September, on receipt of a telegram informing the G.O.C that 9 and 31 Companies, A.S.C., were to be held in readiness to embark for South Africa at an early date. The details required to complete the companies to their establishments were quickly found in volunteers who were most

ABOVE: 32 Company, in Shorncliffe on 26 June 1908 parade to celebrate
the King's birthday. BELOW: Lieut R. T. Snowden-Smith, the first Corps
officer to fly, vaunts his newly acquired aviator's certificate, the 29th
issued by the Royal Aero Club. He survived this dangerous pursuit to
become Director of Supplies and Transport 1940-43.

anxious to leave "Ould Ireland" with a view of active service. As it was rumoured that very little time would be allowed before date of embarkation everyone set to work handing over horses, company equipment, &c., and receiving mobilization equipment, and as the companies have only recently returned from the manoeuvres everyone had plenty to do. The work was well advanced when definite instructions were received that they would embark on the s.s. *Gaul*, at Southampton, on the 17th inst. The G.O.C. inspected the details in the same dress as for embarkation at 12 noon, 15th inst., 9 Coy, being quite proud of being given the opportunity of displaying the gold cross guns previous to their departure. After a very careful inspection the troops were dismissed, and as the hour of departure drew near the square presented a very animated appearance, such as is very seldom seen on the Curragh. The bands of the 6th Dragoons, 2nd Leicester Regiment, and 1st Royal Dublin Fusiliers turned out to give them a befitting send off. Punctually at 3 p.m., to the strains of "Soldiers of Our Queen," the companies fell in, and after being addressed by Lieut.-Col. Oughterson, who complimented them upon their smartness and conduct during their stay at the Curragh. After three hearty cheers for the Commanding Officer, the troops marched to the station, accompanied by the Commanding Officer, Adjutant,, and a large number of friends.

Entertainment at the A.S.C. Theatre, June 1899. The entertainment arranged by Mrs. A. N. Roberts, in aid of the fund for the widows and orphans of soldiers killed on active service in South Africa, was given on November 28th at the Army Service Corps Theatre, and was a complete success. Every seat was filled, many persons having to stand at the sides and end of the hall. The programme was bright, brief, and varied, and the audience was enthusiastic in its appreciation.

Emigrants' Information Office. 31, Broadway, Westminster, S.W. January 1900 — The January Circulars of the Emigrants' Information Office and the Annual Editions of the penny Handbooks show the present prospects of emigration. The Notice Boards are now exhibited, and the Circulars may be obtained free of charge at nearly 500 Public Libraries and Institutions throughout the country.

It is too early in the season for the ordinary emigrant to go to CANADA, unless he has friends to go to or money to keep him till the spring, when there is likely to be the usual demand for competent farm labourers.

In SOUTH AUSTRALIA there has been a demand for farm hands, and for married couples without children for farm station work. There is no demand for more mechanics in Adelaide or elsehere, but miners have been well employed, and there is the usual demand for female servants.

In NEW ZEALAND there has been plenty of employment for men in the building and engineering trades, in the flaxmills and saw-mills, and to a less extent in the boot and clothing trades; competent bushfellers, road makers, farm hands, and shearers have no difficulty getting work in country districts during the present busy season.

With regard to SOUTH AFRICA persons are warned against going there at the present time in search for work.

South Africa, February 1900. There are now over 3000 N.C.O.'s and Men of this Corps serving in South Africa, the long lines of communication and numerous depots make the duties most arduous, but unless this important Branch is efficient the rest of the army must suffer. It is proposed to arrange the work of collecting useful articles into Districts . . . grateful for any contributions such as caps, socks, pocket-handkerchiefs, pipes, tobacco, cigarettes, etc., etc., or monies to purchase them or other comforts.

South Africa, March 1900. The following is taken from The Green Howard's Gazette:- "Though so far from the base (De Aar), we

ABOVE: The MT sheds of 78 Company, the second MT Company of the Corps. ASC steam engine No 83 was purchased in 1910 for £425. BELOW: Early MT course, October 1910: Captain O. Striedinger (with dog) and Captain T. M. Hutchinson (arms crossed) were important personalities in the development of transport in the Army.

have fresh meat daily and fresh bread, which speaks well for the Commissariat arrangements, and we also have a daily ration of tea, sugar, jam, and potatoes."

Mrs. Hill, wife of Sergt. A. E. Hill, 14 Co., A.S.C., has sent the following extract of a letter from her husband:-

"One would not believe the strength of the positions our army has to attack, unless they saw them. We are not fighting Boers, but Europeans of all sorts; but our time will come. We are still trying to relieve Ladysmith. They did not want for anything in the way of food at Christmas time, they received the puddings that were sent, which were greatly appreciated by the men, and are looking forward to the time when they receive the Queen's chocolate."

South Africa, May 1900. Sergt. Hill, A.S.C., sending home his Queen's chocolate on 2nd March, from Ladysmith, says: "Our troops got through on 28th February. It was a hard fight, and the enemy lost heavily. I never heard such an awful shelling before; every gun we had was in action, it must have been a frightful time for the Boers. No one could understand what we have to fight against, unless they were here to see the fortifications against us. General Buller deserves high credit for his work. The troops cheer him every time he passes them." A second letter dated 11th March from Elandslaagte says: "Being Sunday we are resting. We are advancing up country in pursuit of the enemy. We are now about 18 miles from Ladysmith, and the Boers are making a stand about 8 miles in front of us. I am getting used to the hardships, but it is the casualties make us sick. I wonder what bread tastes like; we are still on Bully Beef and Biscuits and Jam, but there is a rumour afloat that we are to have bread by next Christmas, should we have the luck to win and drive the Boers out of our colony. I have seen several Boers come through our camp as prisoners — they are confident they will win, but I am afraid they cannot read their maps properly, or else they have them upside down, because they are going the wrong road to Durban."

The third letter dated 13th March, says: "I am in Ladysmith on duty today, but return to Elandslaagte to-morrow again. I send you Riband and Rosette worn in Ladysmith in commemoration of the relief. The Rosette is Red, White, and Blue, and on the red riband is printed Genl. Buller, V.C., on the blue, Genl. White, V.C., and on the white in large gold letters, Relief of Ladysmith, Feb., 28th 1900."

Supply Depot,
Army Service Corps,
Fourteen Streams
Griqualand West,
South Africa.
25th May, 1900.

Letter to the Editor, July 1900. Sir, Yesterday, the 24th inst., on the anniversary of Our Most Gracious Queen's birthday, an interesting event took place here, and that was the arrival of two cases of comforts kindly forwarded by

ABOVE: Drill squad on 'W' Square in 1910. In the background are the soda pop factory and store, the 'Tramlines' and the waggon bays. BELOW: Christmas dinner layout for 74 and 78 Companies, Aldershot 1910. The Corporal is poised to pour the sherry. (B)

Col. Clayton, Capetown, from friends of the Corps at home. The comforts consisted of woollen underwear and stationery. The feelings of the Detachment, consisting of Nos. 4A and 15 Bakery Sections and Depot Unit, may better be imagined than described, as most of the articles in wear at the present time are just rags, and almost falling off one's back. The nights now are bitterly cold and everyone was in need of warm garments, especially the bakers, whose work even at home is more hot than pleasant at times, whereas in this climate they are doubly scorched during the day, whilst baking, and therefore must feel the cold nights more severely than others. The work of the Corps on all sides has been very heavy and most trying, yet everyone has borne it most cheerfully, and are only too anxious to keep up our past reputation. Trusting the ladies and others who have so thoughtfully contributed towards our comfort will accept our heartfelt thankfulness and good wishes.

I am, Sir,
Yours faithfully
Fred Law, Staff Sergt. Major,
49 Co., A.S.C.

Letter to the Editor, September 1900
20th Company A.S.C. in Action
20th Company,
Army Service Corps,
3rd Cavalry Brigade,
Near Rhenoster.
28th July, 1900.
Dear Atkins,
On July 19th we had a great fight with De Wet. He surrounded our Brigade and pressed his rear attack home. All the men of my company turned out and went into the firing line and behaved very well. The Boers gave us a very warm fire, luckily we had 100 dismounted Cavalry men. I took command of the crowd and occupied a ridge, and taking advantage of a lull in the firing I rushed forward and drove the Boers from a Kopje which commanded us. When I charged, three A.S.C. men, three Australians, and seven dismounted cavalrymen under Baring of the 17th Lancers,

only followed. We drove the Boers from the Kopje and potted them as they were getting on their horses at the other side, and then advanced. Later on we were reinforced by 20 Mounted Rifles under Nichols, and then the Boers shelled us and we had a very hot 20 minutes. We held the Kopje. I saw a Boer 20 yards from me. I lay down and potted him in the stomach. His shot went just over my head. We picked up four dead Boers after the fight besides the man I wounded, and they must have had a lot more. My Quartermaster Sergeant was slightly wounded in the arm. Several of the Boers' shots (Mauser) hit our wagons. It was touch and go that they didn't rush us.

Yours sincerely,
George Vawdrey.

Electricity, Aldershot, January 1902. Aldershot Camp is to be lit by electricity. The Lighting Station has been established close to Thorn Hill, near the spot where the Ordnance Workshops used to stand. An enormously high chimney is the most striking feature in the new buildings. It can be seen for miles round. We hope it will not fall down — at any rate during our generation — or else the Corps might suffer.

Service Dress, February 1902. Introduction of a Service Dress (Regular Forces and Militia). His Majesty the King has been graciously pleased to approve of the introduction of a service dress for wear by the Army.

Peace in South Africa, June 1902. Long before the JOURNAL reaches its readers the whole world will know that Peace in South Africa is now assured. Our longest war of recent years is over; one that cost thousands of valuable lives and many millions of money. The conquered people have been given generous terms, but if these conduce to the Boers settling down in peace, we think the British Army will not grudge our recent enemies what has been conceded to them.

ABOVE: A disgusted horse encounters the 'baby' Hornsby caterpillar during its 10 day journey from Grantham to Aldershot. BELOW: Manoeuvres in East Anglia in 1912, with hired Fodens.

41

Since October, 1899, the Corps has been represented in South Africa by some 250 Officers and about 4,000 W.O.'s, N.C.O.'s, and men. It is not for us to say how we have done our share or what our work has enabled others to accomplish.

On 1st January last we expressed a hope that this year might see peace restored and a large reduction in the number of our comrades serving in South Africa. We rejoice that a measure of our hopes are within easy distance of being fulfilled. We do not lose sight of the fact, however, that the "settling up" of the campaign will entail a great deal of work for the A.S.C., so that the reductions cannot be but gradual.

Journal Subscriptions. Attention is directed to our "Editor's Notes" in this issue which announce various changes in the rates of subscripton etc., to the JOURNAL. Commencing 1st January, 1903, Officers will be charged 4s. a year, the proper price of the paper, insted of 4s 6d., a rate which arose from the postage of each number formerly costing 1d. before the days when 4 ozs. could be sent for one penny. The subscriptions from all members of the Corps who are not Officers, will, from 1st July, 1902, be reduced to three Shillings and Sixpence, if paid yearly in advance, but not under any other circumstances.

Although we have no Regimental District, and consequently no affiliated Volunteer Battalions, we watch with great interest the progress of the A.S.C. Companies, which already form an important part of a few, only too few, Volunteer Brigades.

Colonel ASC, October 1902. Aldershot, the largest station of the Corps (and also, we believe, the largest Lieutenant-Colonel's Command in the whole British Army) tendered its dutiful congratulations to His Royal Highness as follows — vide Detachment Order no. 1940 of 8th September, 1902 — which is worded as follows:-

"On receipt of the information of the appointment of Field Marshal His Royal Highness A. W. P. A. Duke of Connaught and Strathearn, D.C., &, as Colonel of Army Service Corps, the following telegram was despatched to the Aide-de-Camp in waiting to His Royal Highness:- 'Please convey to his Royal Highness the gratification of all ranks at his appointment as Colonel-in-Chief of the Corps.' To which the following reply was received:- 'His Royal Highness, Duke of Connaught, thanks all ranks for kind message. — A.D.C. in Waiting'."

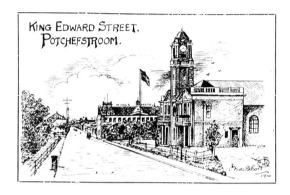

Terms of Service, February 1903. The terms of service for Army Service Corps Drivers have been altered to two years with the Colours and ten years in the Reserve in place of three and nine years respectively. Rendered imperative by the recent large increase to the Corps and the absolute necessity for augmenting the strength of the Transport Reserve we feel confident that there will be no foolish wailing at the difficulty of making a recruit into a driver in such a short space as two years, for it must be remembered, particularly in the Army Service Corps, that necessity has no laws.

First MT Company, March 1903. The first Mechanical Transport Company of the British Army was officially formed on 6th February, a date which marks an important step in the history of the Transport Service. This Company has been numbered 77, as there will eventually be 76 "Horse" Companies.

ABOVE: Sunday Church Parade in Aldershot, 1912. The Corps Church of St George is just visible. (F) BELOW: The Burrell 'small' steam engine, purchased in 1908 for £549; maximum authorised speed: 5 mph.

Corps Week, April 1903. From Monday the 8th until Saturday the 13th of June it is intended to have a general Corps gathering at Aldershot, including two cricket matches, for which the following fixtures have been made:-

Royal Artillery, 10th and 11th.
Royal Engineers, 12th and 13th.

Also every endeavour will be made to fix the Annual Sports for the 6th and 8th. In these Sports there will be a large proportion of events open to competitors from all our other Stations. A Corps Dance will, it is hoped, be arranged for one night during the week. On the last day of the Sports, i.e., 9th June, luncheon will be served in the A.S.C. Theatre to all Officers of the Corps and their families who signify their intention of being present not later that June 1st. It is hoped that this "Corps Week" will be thoroughly supported, and also that the best cricket team the Corps can produce from all home Stations will be got together.

South Africa. The "Army and Navy Gazette" of 4th April contained the following allusion to the work of the Corps in South Africa.

"It is generally admitted that the branch of the Service which came best through the war, all things considered, was the Army Service Corps. Its responsibilities were enormous, but there was no breakdown. It was the first occasion upon which the Corps had been tested on an extensive scale, and the system inaugurated by Sir Redvers Buller may be pointed to as a monument to the great organising ability of that distinguished soldier. So far as field efficiency is concerned there is little in the system of the Corps which could be mended or improved.

Dress: A whisper reaches us from the back of the men's blocks, that the Drivers have been heard to speak of the new Field Service Dress as their "ping-pong" suits.

Corps Week, July 1903. Rain, heavy, persistent, chilly rain, very much marred the first "Corps Week," which was intended to take place here from Monday 8th, to Saturday 13th June. The Annual Athletic Sports were held on the Monday. Although there was a cool wind, the day was fortunately fine. A large number of visitors assembled, and best of all, there was quite a sprinkling of retired officers and members of the Corps of all ranks from several other stations. The day's programme was well carried out, and the crowd of people in the theatre testified to the attractiveness of the Mess President's arrangements in that most useful building.

Corps Band, August 1903. The voluntary Band continues to make such excellent progress that a special measure of congratulation is due to our Bandmaster, Mr. H. J. Cook, late Wiltshire Regt., for his untiring efforts. The members of the Band equally deserve credit from the manner in which they have responded to Mr. Cook's tuition. The Band funds, alas, are not in as flourishing a condition as we would like. Will officers who have not sent their subscriptions kindly do so.

Rations on Manoeuvres, September 1903. After the Manoeuvres are over we hope to supply our readers with a few notes from an Army Service Corps point of view. An item of interest is the introducton for the first time of a "Haversack Ration" consisting of 5 biscuits and 2½ ozs. cheese. The name of this ration clearly shows its object and we are inclined to warmly congratulate its inventor. We are also delighted to notice that "the provision ration counts from the mid-day meal (dinner) of the day of issue, and includes breakfast and the 'Haversack Ration' of the next day."

This point is one which A.S.C. Officers have endeavoured to secure in many past manoeuvres and we welcome the order not only in its bearing on our own work but because it has always appeared to us unreasonable to say "the British soldier is

LEFT: Lieut G. C. G. Blunt (seated left) attended a balloon course in Farnborough in 1906. Colonel Cody, the famous aeronautical pioneer, instructed on the course. RIGHT: King George V visits Malta, c1913. The ASC was responsible for transport arrangements. BELOW: 77 Company detachment in Malta, c1913. Ambulance No 9 is a Leyland and the car is an Arrol-Johnston.

improvident and if you give him food to keep he will either eat it overnight or chuck it away." One of the most important lessons which can be learnt by troops on Manoeuvres is how to look after their rations.

A.S.C. Journal. As may doubtless have been noticed by many of our readers The Army & Navy Gazette of the 15th of August contained the following flattering notice of our Regimental Paper:-

"The Army Service Corps Journal is now quite an established institution, and is evidently receiving from all ranks the support it deserves. It is an admirable military publication, and worthy the corps d'elite whose interests it is its aim to advance. After the events of 1899-1902, the A.S.C. may reasonably claim to take its place side by side with the R.A. and R.E. Never, perhaps, in the wide history of war has any corps had a bigger burden cast upon it and never certainly has any military body more thoroughly justified public confidence from one end of the world to the other. The success of the supply and transport branches in South Africa is referred to with astonishment. This being so, it is to the advantage of our whole Army that the journal before us, which enters now on its twenty-fifth volume, should go on and prosper, as there is fortunately every prospect of its doing."

Furbelows and Frills, August 1904. Electric trams are now running from Woolwich to Bexley Heath: the other day at Welling a lady who had obviously been to a local garden party found that the only vacant seat to be had was between two of our Drivers. For some occult reason best known to herself, she sat down with great care, drawing her furbelows and frills around her so as not to be contaminated by contact with them; her expression however suddenly changed when one said to the other "Bill, let's get off, this ain't no place for clergymens' sons."

Essex Manoeuvres, September 1904. Most of the past month at Aldershot has been taken up by the 1st Army Corps Training, and in preparation for the Manoeuvres which are to take place in Essex in September. This scheme was at the same time interesting and instructive, the general idea being that the Armies of two Foreign Powers had simultaneously effected a landing in England, at Holyhead and the Wash respectively, were marching on London, but had not yet established inter-communications.

The Inspector of the A.S.C. reports that the A.S.C. in London requires more practice in leaping.

Curragh Camp. The Mechanical Transport is in full swing and, though there are many difficulties with bog-roads, they help the horses considerably.

Aldershot Command, November 1904. On the 21st of last month it was announced that in accordance with War Office instructions the area comprised in the Aldershot Military District will in future be known as the "Aldershot Command" in place of the "1st Army Corps".

Camels' Teeth. Thanks to Lieutenant-Colonel G. R. C. Paul, C.M.G., who has recently returned to Chatham from special service in Somaliland, the dentition of the Camel can now be practically studied at the A.S.C. School of Instruction. At very considerable trouble he collected a complete set of camel mouths, showing the condition of the teeth at various ages, and presented these to the School.

ABOVE: 44 Company tug-o-war team at Woolwich, winners of Colonel Horniblow's Challenge Cup in 1912. (E) BELOW: Colonel Cody's funeral procession in August 1913, North Camp. ASC soldiers carried the floral tributes. (B)

Aldershot Manoeuvres. Mechanical Transport was not used with the Blue Force except to convey Bread and Groceries. This form of Transport has considerably improved since our last experience of Manoeuvres at home, and no doubt has a great future, particularly as far as the lorries are concerned. One cannot help mentioning the "Petrol lorries" which, owing to their rapidity, and ease in quickly getting up steam, saved the situation on more than one occasion.

MT Committee, January 1905. Colonel F. T. Clayton, C.B., A.S.C., Assistant Director of Transport, has been appointed president of the committee approved by the War Office to consider the question of how motor power can be utilised for the purpose of transport work in peace and war.

MT Ranks, February 1905. By Army Order 1 of 1905 three new ranks are created in the Mechanical Transport Companies, Army Service Corps — their titles and rates of pay are as follows:- Mechanical Sergeant Major, 7s. a day, Mechanist Quarter Master Sergeant, 6s. a day, and Mechanist Staff Sergeant, 5s. 3d. a day.

Automobile Notes, May 1905. A slight innovation has been made in this number of the "Journal" by the introducton of "Automobile Notes." Now that the Army Service Corps has taken over the general direction, as well as the executive work of the Mechanical Transport of the Army, it would seem that everyone belonging to the Corps should take an intelligent interest in this branch of transport work — a branch which has undoubtedly a great future in front of it.

Found, August 1905. An officer's revolver, left some time or other (probably during or after the South African War) at Cape Town. Application to the Adjutant, A.S.C., The Castle, Cape Town.

Automobile Notes, September 1905. All lamps should be removed from the car if it is necessary to fill up the petrol tanks at night.

No person may drive a motor car unless he be licensed. The fee for a licence is 5s., and it must be renewed annually.

Aldershot Manoeuvres, October 1905. No. 78 Company, under Capt. H. R. Hayter, went out (on manoeuvres) as a unit with engines of various types and sizes as well as lorries of various types. It was encamped as a separate unit under the orders of the A.D. of S. & T. and was kept fully at work distributing equipment, delivering bread and rations, clearing camp, etc. No breakdown of a serious nature occurred, there were no complaints of reckless driving and no delays occurred in delivering at the eight different camps. Anyone who had previously looked "sideways" at Mechanical Transport and who saw the work done on the manoeuvres this year, could not fail to be struck with its value.

A separate camp was formed and all engines or lorries in charge of No. 78 Company that required repair were sent to the shops or Repairing Train, and speedily put right. This train was ready for work at any time of the day or night and the only drawback was that repairs and breakdowns were not frequent enough to keep the artificers as busy as they might have been.

Automobile Notes, December 1905. The successful demonstration, in America, of carrying an apparatus for wireless telegraphy in motor cars, is of military importance, and the day may come when the familiar white and black posts which support the wires of the field telegraph will be seen no more, and the fun (for the enemy) of cutting telegraph wires will be done away with.

Automobile Notes, March 1906. Two 15 h.p. motor cars are shortly expected at Aldershot from the makers, The Wolseley Tool and Motor Car Company, and will be taken over by the A.S.C. The engines of these cars are of the very latest type, four vertical cylinders, mechanically operated inlet valves, high tension magneto ignition, and live axle.

ABOVE: 52 Company relay team, ASC sports winners 1913. Lieut E. H.Fitzherbert is seated. BELOW: Steam engines on their pallet, about to be unloaded from HMS *Commonwealth* in Grand Harbour, Malta, 1913.

Motor bicycles for the use of mechanical transport officers are shortly to be provided.

Automobile Notes, April 1906. In a few years, when automobiles of all kinds become very plentiful, the danger of collision with another motor car round blind corners will be a very real one indeed, and such a contingency can only be avoided by each car keeping strictly to its own side of the road, and slackening speed. Curves to the left can be taken somewhat faster than those to the right.

Bulford Camp, March 1907. A considerable addition to the Mechanical Transport at this station has taken place this month. A Merryweather Motor Fire King, the first to be bought by the War Office, has been placed in charge of this detachment; the engine is similar to those used in London, can travel at the rate of 25 miles an hour, throw a jet of water 150 feet high — 300 gallons a minute.

Stable Belt, June 1907. A slight change in the dress of the Corps has been authorized, and for once officers need be under no apprehension, as it does not entail any addition to their tailor's bills. A web girdle has been introduced to replace the white belt for N.C.O.'s and men of the transport branch. We have not seen the girdle yet, but if it is on the lines of the one worn last year by certain volunteers at Aldershot, it will certainly be a change for the better.

Territorial Notes, June 1908. Aldershot is to be favoured this year by a visit from the Divisional Transport and Supply Columns of the two London Divisions of the Territorial Army.

The Lowland Divisional Transport and Supply Column has the distinction of being the first Territorial Army Service Corps Unit to obtain 30% of its Establishment.

Olympia, August 1910. For the first time on record the Army Service Corps Band made its appearance at the Royal Naval and Military Tournament. They played at both performances on Thursday, Friday and Saturday, the 7th, 8th and 9th of July, and acquitted themselves with credit.

Award of Pensions
7311 S.S.M. C. A. Beach, 48 pence, life.
9897 C.Q.M.S. W. B. Warner, 27 pence, life.
9898 Driver R. Harwood, 12 pence, life.
13128 C.S.M. C. Williams, 20 pence, life.
9891 Sergt. S. J. Biddle, 21 pence, life.
9901 Whr. S. Sergt. T. G. Ellsom, 24 pence, life.
10574 Driver J. Reynolds, 10 pence, life.
9955 S. Sergt. H. C. Fory, 18 pence, life.
29205 Sergt. Master Tailor J. H. Connolly, 20 pence, life.

Royal Flying Corps, April 1913. Sergt Saywood proceeded to the Royal Flying Corps on probation on 20th March. In view of the fact that he has gone as a clerk it came as somewhat of a surprise to us to learn that he is to qualify in flying. Presuming that we were not having our leg pulled, we can only wish him many happy returns — to earth.

The horse: 'I say, they won't want me at all soon, I'm afraid.' The cat: 'Cheer up, old fellow! The mouse-trap didn't do away with me.'

Our Employment Agency. A vacancy exists for a storekeeper in the Mechanical Transport Stores Branch, A.S.C., Aldershot. Wages 30/- per week, rising by triennial increments of 2/- to 40/- per week. Suitable for pensioner W.O. or S.Q.M.S. with good knowledge of accounting. Applications accompanied by copies of testimonials, should be addressed to Commandant, A.S.C. Training Establishment, Aldershot.

ABOVE: Butchers of the Reserve Supply Depôt ASC of the North Midlands Division at annual camp, c1912. BELOW: Men of 49 (West Riding) Division Column scrub webbing at annual camp, 1914.

THE GREAT WAR 1914-1918

Editorial, September-October 1914. We do not think the time is ripe for making many comments on the war, but we cannot but be proud of the good accounts which we are constantly receiving from all sources of the manner in which the A.S.C. are doing their share of the work in the theatre of operations.

We congratulate those members of the Corps who have already been mentioned in despatches, and have no doubt that we may look forward to seeing many more familiar names in despatches of the future.

We seem to have had quite a fair share of actual fighting, and we would certainly like to draw the attention of officers commanding new formations in the armies now being raised to the importance of preparing their men for this part of their work.

The King at Aldershot. Inspection of the New Army. A loyal welcome from all classes. Under less strenuous conditions and with affairs on the Continent in a brighter prospect the visit paid by their Majesties the King and Queen to Aldershot last week-end would have evoked a great popular demonstration of loyalty. As it was the general public gathered in considerable numbers to pay their small but heartfelt tokens of devotion to their Sovereign, but all realised that the time is not for shouting and hat-waving, but for earnest endeavour on everyone's part in this great national crisis. In this respect their visit has had a far reaching effect on the splendid fellows who have flocked by thousands to the colours and are being trained all over the country to take their places in the field with the British Army on the Continent.

Every man of the New Army now making splendid progress towards efficiency in Aldershot and else-where will feel proud of the signal mark of favour accorded to the whole force by his Majesty the King, who paid a long visit to Aldershot to inspect the divisions under training in the Command, and to see them at work. The visit had been arranged, as announced in these columns some few weeks ago, but had been postponed owing to the pressure of State affairs

A Lucky Escape From Uhlans. The supply and requisitioning officers in their cars have to work on the front and flanks of the main bodies of the troops; much of the work is done at night, and considerable risks have to be run from small detached or scouting parties of the enemy. One morning in the dawning light and in a thick mist a car ran into an outpost of Uhlans, muffled up in their heavy cloaks and half asleep. Before they realized that the car was British it had been smartly turned round and vanished again into the mist.

Wishing you a happy Christmas.

If der A. S. C. haf gone by, den I kan kom out.

On September 10 in daylight a car with two officers and the chauffeur ran suddenly round a corner into four German infantry men. It was too late to turn the car, so one of the officers immediately sprang out and, drawing his revolver, advanced towards the party. In very good English one of them informed the officer that they had already surrendered. One of the men was shot through the lower part of the leg, and was being attended to by a British chaplain attached to the Cavalry

LEFT: London omnibuses on the Western Front, 1914, requisitioned for troop-carrying duties. (G) RIGHT: An armoured lorry, with ASC driver, Margate 1915. (G) BELOW: The supply of the BEF through Boulogne.

Brigade. On the same date 40 Germans surrendered to a small party of A.S.C. of the 3rd Divisional Train. (The Times, Friday, October, 2nd, 1914.)

Subscriptions and Comfort Needed. Mrs. Galloway will be sending parcels containing cigarettes, tobacco, briar pipes, bootlaces, handkerchiefs, socks, etc., to the men of the A.S.C., at present at the war, and if there is anyone belonging to the Corps who wishes to send things to our men, she will be glad to include them, if they are forwarded to her, carriage paid.

The Charge of the Lorry Brigade, November-December 1914. There is a popular impression that the men of the transport service spend their lives in the rear of the fighting line and that they have little share in the adventures of the troops in battle. It is true that they are more in the rear than most other arms of the Service, and their work is more useful than romantic, but nevertheless there are plenty of men in the Army Service Corps who can tell stories of tight corners and narrow escapes which they seem as a rule to thoroughly enjoy.

I have heard during the last few days several accounts of the various adventures these fellows meet with, told by ex-motor-omnibus drivers, and others. One of them was a thrilling charge made by half a dozen heavy lorries quite recently, and was related to me by one of the men who took part in it. This man was driving one of a column of heavy ammunition wagons up the firing line. The officer in command thought there was no chance of the whole convoy escaping, but saw a sporting chance of getting through with some of it. He ordered all the men on to the first half-dozen lorries and took the wheel of the first one himself. They had acted promptly, but the enemy had lost no time, and it was a race between the horses and the wagons. The horses won, and the men of the convoy could see them lining the road and preparing a gauntlet for them to run. The

forlorn hope moved on, however the wagons lumbered along at their dizziest speed and bore down on the waiting cavalry. Rifles cracked and spat; bullets drummed and whistled. "I ducked my head and stamped on the accelerator," said the man who told me the story, "and we simply sailed through them. They didn't hit one of us, but it was a warm time while it lasted. Then they tried to chase us, but soon gave it up. My old cart never went so fast in her life."

THE SINEWS OF WAR.

Private Atkins: 'For what we have received — and are going to receive — here's to the A.S.C.'

Transport Stamina. If we never come into contact with civilization again for six months we could still keep going, except for petrol. Two wagons carry petrol and they always get a fresh supply when going through a town. In the very severe weather that we had a few days ago, of course, we had to empty all radiators when stopped for any length of time. However, several cars had cracked cylinders brazed by the oxygen process by our

ABOVE: Horse-drawn ambulance, Gallipoli. The drivers are ASC. (G)
BELOW: There's nothing like a shave, even late in the day, to make a
keen motor cyclist feel better, Salonika. (G)

own men, and are now in running order again. The remainder of the wagons to the number of about 80 are all loaded up with ammunition of all kinds. My particular car has 40 boxes of 47 shrapnel on and three fuse-boxes. Each box weighs about 130 lb. (The Times, 12th December, 1914.)

News from the Front, February 1915. A member of the A.S.C. Mechanical Transport writes:-

Our company consists of 98 lorries, and this includes two store wagons, three first-aid lorries, breakdown cars, one office and two repair workshops. The two travelling workshops are wonders, and are in duplicate. They are fitted with electric light, and have on board lathes, drilling, and boring and slotting machines, electric riveters, forges, anvils, and everything required in a workshop, even melting pots for running Babbitt's metal in the worn-out bearings before being turned up afresh. The machines are driven by a motor which is driven by a small motor engine. There are other wagons which carry heavy stuff such as portable forges, two or three grindstones, spare springs for cars, crowbars, jacks and heavy tools, and hundreds of other things.

Letters from the Front. An officer of the Army Service Corps writes:-

I don't think I have told you much about what sort of work we do. Of course, we carry ammunition, as you see by our address; but we carry other things besides, such as sandbags, bomb-making materials, consisting of gun cotton, detonators, primer, etc. These we take as a rule direct to the Engineers, which gives us the chance of getting much nearer the front than when carrying ammunition, as the latter we fetch from railhead and deliver to the divisional ammunition column, which is generally a considerable distance behind the firing line.

An officer of the Army Service Corps in a recent letter says: Our Brigade has suffered heavily in the severe fighting, and some of the

very best fellows, with whom we were dining on the previous night, have fallen on Hill 60. Never in my life do I wish to hear such a terrible shaking of the earth as we are experiencing now, and still less do I want to see such awful, unmentionable sights as I saw at Ypres three days ago. Thank God, I got my supply section out without casualty. I recommended two of our fellows for

TOMMY.
on Transport Work.

conspicuous coolness and courage. Our wagons were used for the conveyance of dead and wounded to the hospitals.

The Army Service Corps Prisoners of War Fund. It is proposed to open a "Prisoners of War Fund" for the benefit of those members of the Army Service Corps who are interned in Germany. There are some sixty prisoners of war so situated, and up till now they have been looked after in a most generous and public-spirited way by Lady Burghclere who

ABOVE: Women of the Forage Corps (ASC) load bales of hay on the Home Front. (G) BELOW: A Foden de-lousing lorry, January 1917. Clothing was steamed to kill lice, but the eggs seemed to survive. (G)

has up to the present, without the smallest assistance from the Corps, devoted great energies and considerable sums of money which she has herself given and collected from her friends in the endeavour to ameliorate the condition of our unfortunate comrades.

Fickle Tommy! March - April 1915. Aldershot Gazette, 2nd February 1915. An officer, part of whose duty it is to censor the letters of his men, tells an amusing story of how he succeeded in reducing his labours in this direction. Incidently he explains why anxious relatives — and those who aspire to that distinction — do not always receive as much news from the front as they would like. The officer is Lieutenant C Smallpiece, and this is his story:-

"For some time the section of the Army Service Corps of which I am in command was sent to rest at a base, and it became part of my duties to censor all the letters which the men wrote home. They had nothing else to do but to write letters, and the censoring became a very serious business for me, as I frequently had at night to wade carefully through 150 love-letters. So I decided to introduce a change, if possible, and one day I motored into Boulogne and bought a football, which I took back for my men to play with. The result was quite marvellous. The money I spent for the football proved the best investment I ever made. The men took to it so keenly that they played football all day, and had very little time left in which to write love-letters. After the introduction of the football I never had more than five love-letters to censor at night".

Socks, March - April 1915. A dear old lady has indignantly refused to knit anything more for our soldiers, since she read in a Tommy's letter that "our chaps are giving the Germans socks."

A Driver's Life. There may not be much pleasure in the life led by the driver of the motor lorry; but those who imagine that he leads an uneventful humdrum existence or that the Army Service Corps is a non-combatant branch of the Army should hear the experience of some of these men. They included early in the war many narrow escapes from hostile cavalry patrols, long night journeys without lights over bad roads between the hostile lines, daily drives over the open stretch of a plateau swept by howitzer shell, and generally exhausting days and sleepless nights spent in taking up food and carrying back wounded. Even under present conditions the work is arduous and not always free from danger. It will then be realized that there is as much romance and excitement and as much opportunity for heroism in driving a lorry as there is in seemingly more adventurous duties. (The Times, 11th March, 1915.)

Don't look a gift horse in the mouth.

Army Service Corps Comforts Fund

Somewhere in France,
Dear Madam,   29th June, 1915.
I have very much pleasure in writing to you, on behalf of No. 2 Co, A.S.C., Horse Transport, Meerut Divisional Train, and thanking you and your kind friends for the splendid parcels which you have so kindly sent out to us. They were received in perfect condition; not one had been tampered with; and what's more were received at a very appropriate moment, as we had been having it a bit rough for the past few days, in a deluge

ABOVE: Water tanks on American built 'FWD' lorries. (G) BELOW: A Holt caterpillar tows an artillery howitzer. The ASC pulled all heavy guns during the Great War. (G)

of rain, and the spirits of our lads were almost as gloomy as the weather.

But when the parcels were distributed, the change was remarkable; it put one in mind of a "school treat," or the after effects of a "Father Christmas." The boys (for really, some of them are not much more) were highly delighted, and kept going from one to another, asking, "What have you got, Bill, in yours? I've got a khaki shirt, etc. (proper swankey one too) in mine." "Oh! I've got a safety razor, and a blooming fine pocket book, etc., in mine, it's just what I wanted." "I'm not cribbing." And so on.

It is indeed very kind of you, dear madam, and all the good people at home, to send us out these little comforts, which I can assure you are very highly appreciated by all of us; it keeps the spirits of the men up, and helps every one of us "to do our little bit" with a good heart.

Once more thanking you and your kind friends for thoughts of our welfare,

I remain,
Yours very gratefully,
C. S. WILKS, C.S.M.,
No. 2 Co., A.S.C., M.D. Train

Comforts Fund. The Army Service Corps Comforts Fund for Horse Transport and Supply Branches of the Corps was started by Mrs Landon, 4K Portman Mansions, W, in September 1914, and with the assistance of lady friends. 9,247 parcels have been packed and forwarded oversea up to the present date.

The parcels were distributed as follows:- Divisional trains, 6,018; Reserve Parks (Railhead Supply Detachments, etc), 3,229. 4th Corps Railhead, British Expeditionary Force, 28th May, 1915.

Madam. Your parcel of 27 presents duly arrived, and was distributed to the men at the Railhead. The men were very pleased indeed, and the ones that benefited were A.S.C. and R.E. postal men. All the men at this most exposed Railhead have been out since August and through the thick of it, and I may tell you your present is the very first we have ever received; so you see the poor A.S.C. men are not as lucky as their brother soldiers. The men wish me to thank you and all the other good ladies who sent them out the comforts.

They also wish you many happy years. And God bless you.

Your truly,
Neville Leese
Major, A.S.C.

The Army Service Corps Prisoners of War Fund, September - October 1915. All our prisoners of war in Germany are extremely grateful for the parcels of food, etc, which the fund sends to them regularly once a week, and shoals of postcards have been received from them, one and all containing nothing but praise and thanks for the good things that have been sent out to Germany for their use.

I AM A DRIVER IN THE A.S.C.

The following is a total list of articles which have been despatched up to the 23rd October:-

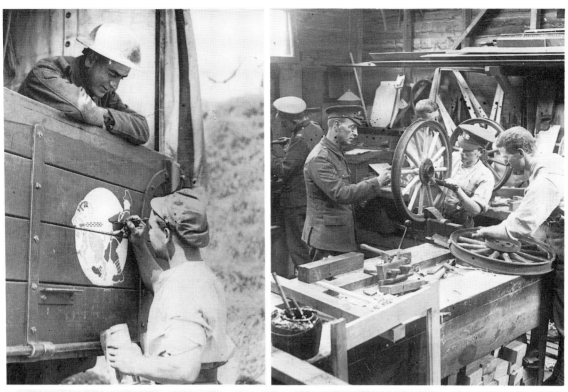

LEFT: Painting the unit sign of 26 Siege Battery Ammunition Column: the ASC led the Army in introducing unit signs on vehicles. (G) RIGHT: ASC workshop wheelers at work. (G) BELOW: A typical rations dump on the Western Front. (G)

680 Malt Loaves
671 lbs. Jam
311 lbs. Granulated Sugar
490 lbs. Butter
126 lbs. Chocolate
126 lbs. packets Chocolate
361 tins Milk
439 Cheeses
368 tins Cocoa and Milk
56 tins Herrings
186 tins Golden Syrup
184 tins Corned Beef
100 packets Milk
489 packets Soup
621 packets Tea
489 packet Peas
310 packets Muscatels
451 2-oz packets Tobacco
3123 packets Cigarettes
56 packets Toilet Paper
186 packets Tooth Powder
348 packets Lemon
360 packets Wheatmeal Rations
190 lbs Marmalade
122 tins Pineapple
122 tins Veal and Ham
122 Lunch Tongues
248 Chicken and Ham galantine
198 packets Biscuits
69 Potted Loaves
122 tins Peppermint Bulls Eyes
489 Tablets Soap
817 Sausages
184 Tinder Lighters
43 Pipes
3 Sets Dominoes
121 pairs Shoes
199 pairs Socks
173 Flannel Shirts
56 Tooth Brushes
56 Khaki Handkerchiefs
117 Towels
137 Books
5 packets Frozoctone
69 packets Insect Powder
69 Housewives
32 Games
64 pairs Trousers
124 Vests

127 Cardigans
124 pairs Pants
4 Pyjamas
59 pairs Braces
2 pairs Gloves
1 Cricket Ball

How Soldier Decoyed Huns, November - December 1915. It was reported at a meeting of the Wood Green (London) District Council recently that a Wood Green man, Corporal A Clack, of the A.S.C. has just been awarded the French Medaille Militaire for bravery. Clack showed the utmost resourcefulness in drawing a body of Germans straight into the French lines. He was alone on horseback when he observed a helmet and coat of an enemy soldier on the ground, and he promptly put them on. The Germans were advancing and he rode up to them and assumed the leadership until he had enticed them all safely into the hands of the French. (Daily Mail, 26th November, 1915.)

Alexandra Pavilion, January - February 1916. The Alexandra Pavilion for Officers, 52 Grosvenor Gardens (opposite Victoria Station) S.W. For the use of officers in uniform. Open day and night. Club Room; Bedrooms; Bath rooms. Charge for Bedroom, Bath, Breakfast, valeting, &c. 4/- Without Breakfast, 2/6. Telegraph Address:- Swordback, Sowest, London. Phone:- Victoria, 2696.

Xmas Festivities. Aldershot, January - February 1916. The Army Service Corps had, as usual, a very large number of men in mess, and each company decorated its dining room more or less. There was less time than usual spent on ornamenting the walls.

The one exception was the hut used by the men of the "Caterpillar" Section as a general dining room. This had been very prettily decorated with evergreens and paper festoons, which were skilfully arranged over the ceilings and walls, whilst here and there were mottoes worked in gold and white paper wishing the season's greetings to the officers

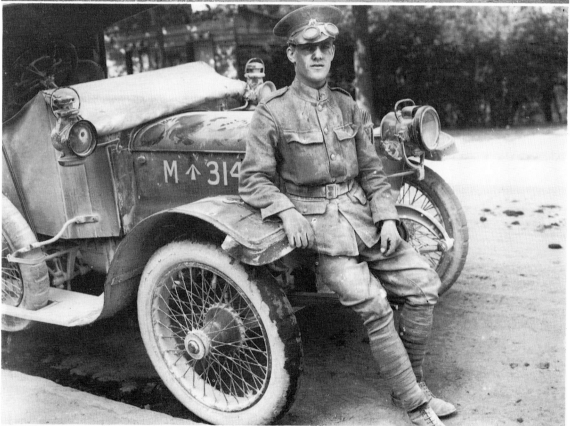

ABOVE: The casualty reception park of an ASC Workshop. BELOW: Clearly goggles were an essential part of an ASC car driver's ensemble.
(G)

of the section. At night, when the lights were on, the effect was very pleasing.

As is customary in the corps, the sergeants devoted themselves to ensuring the comfort and enjoyment of their men on Christmas day, and in each company the Officer Commanding paid a welcome visit at the dinner hour to the men, there being the customary exchange of hearty good wishes, and the toasting of healths.

Distinguished Conduct Medal, March - April 1916. MS-3943 Acting Corporal E. A. Hellmuth, Army Service Corps (attached Royal Engineers) — For conspicuous gallantry. He took his C.O. in a car, and was told not to go back empty, but to fill up with wounded. This he did, but without any orders returned four times for more wounded. He had each time to pass over a road which was being heavily shelled, and to pass through a burning town. His coolness under fire and readiness for any dangerous work are remarkable. He has been wounded.

Distinguished Conduct Medal, March - April 1916. 30240 Driver F. Sutcliffe No. 2 Company Divisonal Train, Canadian A.S.C. — For conspicuous gallantry; he took wagons, loaded with bombs, to various infantry units along the trenches, under very heavy shell fire.

MT Organisation in London, May - June 1916. The underground tire stores would be one of the sights of London if sightseers were permitted there. It recalls the champagne cellars of Rheims, and in a photograph it would appear even more striking than these. It covers an area of 2½ acres, is radiantly clean, deliciously cool, and brilliantly lighted with electricity. Street after street, avenue after avenue, the greatest collection of tires in the world, extend north, south, east and west in symmetrical order. At one point — near 25th Street and 2nd Avenue, for they are all named — you can look through a kind of Morris tube of 300ft. formed of tires set side by side on end. Here there are always in reserve

sufficient tires to supply all the motor vehicles — lorries, cars and bicycles — in the British Army, and 4,000 will be sent out in one day. (The Times, 28th April, 1916.)

War Office and Women Chauffeurs, July - August 1916. Since last August, when Lady Londonderry started the Women's Legion to supply trained women cooks to the home camps and convalescent hospitals, about 2,000 have been successfully employed. The formation of a motor-transport section of the Women's Legion in April of this year has had similarly successful results, and it is now officially recognised by the War Office as a civilian subordinate branch.

The Commandant of this section of the Women's Legion has been in Serbia with the Red Cross and has driven a motor-transport for some weeks at the front. She hopes to obtain for the work women who may have to earn their own living after the war and who would find a congenial occupation in the driving of light vans. Already about 200 women have been placed, not all in War Office work, but some in munition areas, and some working for hospitals. All the expenses of training both the camp cooks and the motor transport section are covered by a private fund subscribed by Lady Londonderry's personal friends. Training for the motor-transport section is given free at certain garages and motor schools with which the Legion has made arrangements.

The work done for the War Office so far has been in connection with the Army Service Corps. The women drive light cars only, and

ABOVE: Women at War: ASC badged drivers enjoy MT training. The
Corporal is perhaps wondering what his wife will think of this picture!
BELOW: Learning repair work on Fowler steam engines. (G)

are drafted in to service units for home service. The Army Council were asked in April to try the women for a month; they agreed, and during the month's test the women were given cars which could not even be described as second-best. The women, however, accepted all difficulties as part of their test, and it was reported that their work was "excellent" and that in many cases the cars were kept cleaner than they had been by the men.

Military Cross, November - December 1916. Second Lieutenant, (Temporary Lieutenant,) Charles Edward Murray Pickthorn, A.S.C. Special Reserve and R.F.C. — For conspicuous gallantry and devotion to duty in attacking hostile aircraft, and in carrying out difficul reconnaissances. One one occasion, although wounded, he continued his combat and brought down a hostile machine. On two other occasions he brought down hostile machines in flames.

Distinguished Conduct Medal, May - June 1917. T/14586 Lance-Corporal, (A/Sergeant,) L. Makin, A.S.C., — For conspicuous gallantry and devotion to duty. He rendered most valuable services with Trench Tramway Detachment in taking up ammunition and supplies.

Military Cross, January-February 1918. Temp, 2nd Lieut. (temp Lieut.) Thomas Noel Heath Stretch, A.S.C. attd. M.G. Corps — For conspicuous gallantry and devotion to duty when in command of a section of machine-guns. He successfully brought his four guns up to the objective with the assaulting infantry, and, finding that the right flank of the brigade was exposed, pushed two guns forward, and was able to bring covering machine-gun fire to bear while the brigade was advancing upon their final objective. He captured two prisoners, and led an infantry bombing party to clear the trench of the remainder of the enemy.

Somewhere in France, January - February 1918. Christmas at the Base M.T. Depôt (Northern) was celebrated by the men for the third year in truly seasonable fashion, mirth and merriment being paramount the whole day through.

The dining hall was resplendent with mistletoe bough and red-berried holly gleaming among festoons of Chinese lanterns and paper chains; the decorative scheme being in the hands of a committee of men who were responsible for the day's festivities.

Much arduous work fell upon the shoulders of the C.Q.M.S. who superintended the catering in first-class style of all the meals more particularly the dinner, when succulent turkeys, various seasonable vegetables, and a free ration of good old-fashioned Xmas puddings were washed down by copious draughts of English beer.

A meed of praise is due to the W.A.A.C.'s, the cooks and waitresses (hence the mistletoe presumably), to these a hearty vote of thanks was accorded upon the proposition of Lieut-Col. G. C. G. Blunt, D.S.O. (Officer Commanding), who was present at the commencement of the dinner with the other Officers of the depot.

Work at the Front, March - April 1918. The following is extracted from Mr Hamilton Fyfe's description of the operations on the Western Front, which appeared in the "Daily Mail" dated 17th April, 1918.

"While I am on this topic I must pay tribute to the way in which our transport services have worked all through this difficult time. If

ABOVE: The ASC Fire Brigade in the Base MT Depôt, Calais. The vehicle is a Commer. BELOW: DIY, Army-style.

it is hard for an advancing army to be fed and provided with ammunition, the task is far harder when a retreating army is concerned. Yet I have heard scarcely a single complaint on this score, and I am sure there is no case in which our men have not had all that was possible done for them.

I met an officer in the Army Service Corps a day or two ago who was with a motor transport section attached to artillery. The duty of the section was to move the guns with lorries and "caterpillars," and also to take up the ammunition. The night before he had been taking shells up through an enemy barrage, "worse than being in a battle," he said, "because you haven't the moral support of others. You are on your own."

The A.S.C. men who carry up the rations to the points where divisional quartermasters take them over are often in tight places too. They were sometimes, even in trench warfare; now they run almost as much risk as anybody. It is like a daily miracle to see the men getting their food so regularly through roads filled with traffic and often under shell fire. The A.S.C. lorries make their way punctually at the appointed hours whatever is happening. I see at noon meals being got ready, cooking going on over little roadside fires, meat being cut up, groups of men sitting round savoury messes or eating their cold "bully" with good appetite if they have to depend upon their iron rations which means tinned food. The working of our quarter-master's department cannot be too highly praised."

The Army Service Corps Prisoners of War Fund, March - April 1918. Provision Parcels. — We are allowed to despatch to each prisoner in Germany every fortnight three Provision parcels of the weight of 10 lbs. each including packing. The Standard Parcels now being sent contain:-

Parcel No. 1 (despatched once a fortnight).
1 lb. tin Army Rations (Meat and Vegetables).
1 lb tin Butter Beans and Tomato Sauce.
1 lb. tin Herrings in Oil.

1 lb. tin Tripe and Onions.
½ lb. tin Meat Paste.
½ lb. Beef Dripping.
¼ lb. Coffee.
1 lb. Rice.
½ lb. Biscuits.
2 Foster Clark's Soup Squares.
2 oz. Tablet Soap.

Drawn by]   **Category "L3."**   [*J. E. Murphy*

Parcel No. 2 (despatched twice a fortnight):-
1 lb. tin Beef
1 lb. tin Butter Beans and Tomato Sauce.
1 lb. tin Herrings in oil.
1 lb. Sausages and Onions.
½ lb. tin Meat Paste.
½ lb. tin Jam.
¼ lb. Tea.
½ lb. Sugar.
½ lb. tin Nestle's Sweetened Condensed Milk.
1 lb. Rolled Oats.
½ lb. specially prepared Pea Soup and Bacon.
2 oz. Tablet Soap.
1 lb. Bacon is substituted for the tin of Herrings once a month.
¾ lb. Cheese is sent twice a month in place of the Butter Beans.

LEFT: Repairing inner tubes in the Base MT Depôt, Rouen, May 1918.
(G) RIGHT: A tired ASC Corporal rests on the Merville road during the
German offensive of 1918. (G) BELOW: LGOC lorries are loaded with
supplies by Chinese members of the Labour Corps, which had its origins
in the ASC in 1914.

In addition to the above, we enclose monthly in one of our parcels:-

1 tin Tooth Powder.

1 small stick Shaving Soap.

1 stick Parasitox (Insecticide).

¼ lb. tin Curry Powder.

The total number of Parcels despatched during the year was 4,110.

Victoria Cross, May - June 1918. For most conspicuous bravery and devotion to duty. Owing to an enemy attack, communications were cut off, and wounded could not be evacuated. The road was reported impassable, but Private Masters volunteered to try to get through, and after the greatest difficulty succeeded, although he had to clear the road of all sorts of debris. "He made journey after journey throughout the afternoon over a road consistently shelled and swept by machine-gun fire, and was on one occasion bombed by an aeroplane. The greater part of the wounded cleared from this area were evacuated by Pte. Masters, as his was the only car that got through during this particular time."

Distinguished Conduct Medal, May - June 1918. M2-177455 Pte. G. Kirkbright, A.S.C. — For conspicuous gallantry and devotion to duty. This driver used excellent judgment in his choice of a route over very treacherous sand dunes during an attack on enemy fortifications. After the enemy redoubts had been attacked in succession, he was instrumental in bringing the Tank back to safety in spite of the severe injuries which he sustained from shell fire, and that the remaining members of the crew were wounded. His coolness and gallantry deserve the highest praise.

Distinguished Conduct Medal. M2-182297 Private, actg. Corporal, J. Ramsey, A.S.C. — For conspicuous gallantry and devotion to duty while in charge of caterpillars moving guns to a forward position. The road was very heavily shelled. Several casualties were caused among his men, and one of the caterpillars was damaged by a shell. This he repaired under very heavy fire. The road was badly broken up; but by skilful manoeuvring he got the gun forward to its position. He then returned to bring another gun forward, but his only caterpillar was put out of action by a shell, whereupon he returned for another, and succeeded in removing the damaged one. He showed great initiative and determination.

S.Sergt. (R.R.) (to A.S.C. Cadet who persistently rises in his saddle at the jumps):- Now then, sir, where are you going to? You're not in the Flying Corps.'

The Osterley Aeroplane, July - August 1918. The Mechanical Transport Training Depot, Isleworth, was a scene of great happenings on August 10th. On that day the annual sports were held, but the *piece de resistance* of the afternoon was the christening, by H.R.H., Princess Patricia of Connaught, of an aeroplane to be named after the Depot. This aeroplane had been purchased out of War Savings subscribed by the men of the Depot through their Association.

Evil-Minded Army Mules, November December 1918. Returning from the O.P. on a misty and muddy morning, I met two mules taking four A.S.C. men for a walk. When I arrived the party had halted before a plank bridge thrown across one of the evil-looking, nasty-smelling ditches to be found only in Flanders during the wet season. The mules

ABOVE: 'Aldershot ovens' at a field bakery, Salonika. (G) BELOW: Huntley & Palmer biscuits galore in an Expeditionary Force Canteen storehouse in Cologne. This forerunner of the NAAFI was an ASC responsibility. (G)

were looking at the bridge and the men were looking at the mules. They had been engaged in this occupation, I learned, for three and a half hours.

"Can I be of any assistance?" I inquired, prompted more by curiosity than sympathy.

"You can", replied one of the clay bipeds fervently. "You can take these unmentionable mules and have them shot, drowned or gassed, or you can keep 'em and take 'em home to play with the children."

"It's no use, Herbert," whined another clay man. "He's no use; it would take a blooming army corps to move these mules. We're here for the duration, we are."

"Can't you push them over?" I suggested.

The first speaker looked at me pityingly. "Push 'em over!" he echoed bitterly.

"Let him try, Herbert," said the other. "Another little push won't do them any harm."

Nettled by the tone rather than by the words, I placed my shoulder against the near-side mule and shoved. The wretched animal did not resist and merely sat down, and I pitched forward full length in the mud. The other animal never took its eyes from the plank bridge.

The men did not laugh as they helped me to my feet. By the bored expression on their faces I gathered that the performance was more monotonous than amusing.

Then the four men individually and in chorus gave me the black record of that pair of mules. They were actually the cleverest and hardiest mules in the service, but so burdened with original sin that their virtues were lost in the shadow of their crimes. Both had carried ammunition through a barrage without blinking or faltering; both had gone farther with heavier burdens than any other pair of mules in the corps; and neither was to be trusted to do a straight-forward job in a straight-forward way.

"It's not as if they were frightened of the bridge," explained one of the weary escort. "They would cross a mountain torrent on a tight-tope if they were in the mood. It's just their mulishness. My opinion is that the blighters have made a bet with each other as

to which shall be the first to move, and nothing short of a land-mine will shift 'em. Cordite (the one you shoved) was the only survivor of a score of mules that got in the way of a shell the other day. He dropped, and we thought he had gone. But when the fragments stopped dropping Cordite raised his head

Wishing you a Happy Christmas.

Hurrah for the A. S. C.

Lawrence Colborne

cautiously, looked round deliberately for any more shells, then scrambled to his feet without so much as a scratch. Lyddite (his partner in crime) has been knocked down by a 'caterpillar,' and it was the 'caterpillar' that needed attention.

I walked in front of the mules and regarded them with deepened interest. Their eyes were fixed on the plank bridge in a stare as uncompromising as truth, as immutable as fate, and I drew away in awe from the vision of stark finality.

When I left the four A.S.C. men the mud was slowly drying on their clothes, and their faces were the faces of men for whom hope is dead. (J. D. Daily Mail, Nov. 14, 1917.)

ABOVE: GS waggons pass the body of a German lorry, gratefully used by British Tommies, March 1918. (G) BELOW: A Holt caterpillar tows a Dennis through the mud of Kempton Park at the end of the war. The race-course was used as the Home Base MT Depôt during the war. (G)

Royal Title, December 1918. His Majesty the King has been graciously pleased to confer the title of "Royal" upon the Army Service Corps in appreciation of the valuable services of this Corps during the War.

In announcing His Majesty's gracious appreciation, the Quarter Master General to the Forces desires to congratulate all ranks of the Army Service Corps on the high honour conferred upon them, and, in doing so, he recalls with pleasure the recent remarks of His Royal Highness the Colonel of the Corps bearing witness to the importance of the services rendered by the Army Service Corps throughout the War. Much of the arduous work done by the Corps in connection with the rearward services and remote from the dangers of the fighting zones. On the other hand, the Field Units of the Army Service Corps are freqently exposed to the gravest dangers in bringing up supplies of food and ammunition to the fighting troops.

In all circumstances the Corps has done its duty, nor can the Quarter Master General recall one single instance where the maintenance of the Troops in any part of the world has failed, thus establishing a record of which the whole Army may be justly proud.

A. Crofton Atkins

War Office   Major General,

29th November, 1918.   Director of

Supplies and Transport.

North-West Frontier, June 1919. Mechanical Transport is employed in taking Supplies, etc., from the neighbourhood of Peshawar, through the Khyber Pass (neutral territory), to the vicinity of the troops working in Afghanistan.

It is just possible to get out and home before dusk, after which the Pass is not safe, and it is a long day's work, with a temperature of 110° in the shade, and increasing daily.

In the Pass itself, we get sniped daily by individual tribesmen; these people are all armed with rifles and continually on the look out for loot.

Reindeer Transport. Whatever the history of the expedition to Northern Russia, one page must be reserved for the achievements of the Reindeer Transport, which was organized to circumvent the vagaries of the railway, the unfailing stupidity of the Russian railway worker when he strives after the elusive ideals of Lenin, and the weather.

Women's Legion, Plans for Permanent Status, February 1920. The demobilization of the motor section of the Women's Legion and the first occasion on which its Reserve has been called upon (during the railway strike) were celebrated by a gathering held at the invitation of the president, Lady Londonderry, at the Londonderry House, Park-lane, the 16th December 1919.

The Passing of the Horse Transport.

"Ole Bill". At 1 p.m. on February 14th a Motor-bus, No. B.43, in the London General Omnibus Company's service, was inspected by His Majesty the King in the Quadrangle at Buckingham Palace. The ceremony was brief but exceedingly interesting. Facing the door of the Palace, through which His Majesty entered the quadrangle, was drawn up a party of 40 employees of the London General Omnibus Company in double rank.

Berlin, The new "Military Government," which suddenly made its appearance in Berlin, is far from popular. All allied troops are more or less confined to their respective working centres. This, together with hardly any lights, no water and a scarcity of foodstuffs and fuel, do not make one's lot a happy one.

ABOVE: Pushball at Woolwich in 1919: players are LCpl Francis, LCpl Chapman, LCpl Mosley, LCpl Clark and SSM Pearson. BELOW: The NAAFI Sports Van visits units on manoeuvres, 1922.

End of the War. By an Order in Council, January 10, 1920, has been fixed as the end of the war with Germany. The date of the termination of the war as a whole has yet to be fixed by Order in Council, and will not be announced until the last of the peace treaties is ratified.

New Waterproof for Officers. The new approved pattern is of waterproof drab cotton twill with two removable linings, one of fleece and one of oil skin. It is double-breasted reaching to the knees, and is fitted with a belt of same material, fastening with a buckle. Metal badges of rank are worn on the shoulder straps. It is an optional garment and not worn in any order of dress.

Danzig. On 26th January, 1920, a small advance party consisting of 6 officers, including the A.D.S. & T., and Supply Officer, and 8 other ranks, left Cologne, and after spending most of the 27th in Berlin, arrived at Danzig early on the 28th. The railway station at Danzig was gay with bunting welcoming home the German prisoners of war, but our welcome was a very cold one, not to mention the atmosphere which registered 17 degrees of frost. After walking a considerable distance in search of officers billets, we came to a German barracks, on the gate of which was a sentry in sheepskin coat, and there the other ranks were quartered. As a German battalion was also accommodated in the barracks, we did not feel too comfortable, especially as some of the "Jerries" made some very unpleasant remarks to us, using choice expressions picked up possibly during their term in England as prisoners of war.

Marriage Allowance Rates, January 1921. An Army Order fixes the rates of marriage allowance for warrant officers, non-commissioned officers and men for the year April, 1921, to March, 1922, at those shown under the figure 160 in the sliding scale issued with Army Order 357 of 1920. These range

from 9s. 6d. for a wife only to 44s. 6d. for a wife and seven children, and 3s. for each additional child.

Rugby Club, November 1921. Rugby enthusiasts will be glad to hear that a Corps Rugby Club has now been formed. The fixture list, so far arranged, is not too ambitious, but when the new club has been more firmly established this state of affairs can, no doubt, easily be remedied.

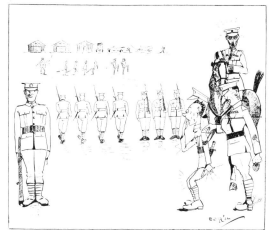

DRILL CERTIFICATES or The Predicament of a Sergeant who found he had one man over.

Clothes & Boots Wanted. Readers who have clothes or wearing apparel of any sort, including boots, for which they have no further use, are asked to send same to the Secretary, R.A.S.C. Compassionate Fund, Kensington Palace Barracks, W.8, for distribution amongst unemployed ex-R.A.S.C. men, many of whom are badly in need of clothes and boots. Parcels sent by rail can be marked "carriage forward."

Carden Car, July 1922. For Sale. — 1921 Carden, fitted with electric light. New Dunlops on back wheels. Engine recently over-hauled. Car in excellent condition. Price, £75. Apply "C," c/o Editor.

MT Establishments, August 1922. It is officially stated that the Local Auxiliary Mechanical Transport Companies, Royal

ABOVE: No 9 Long Transport and Artificer Instructors' Course in Aldershot, 1930, with Vauxhall. BELOW: Bare back wrestling, confidence training for new riders. The horses' views are not recorded.
(H)

Army Service Corps, in Great Britain, will, as from August 1st, be reorganised on a peace basis of four "higher" and 14 "lower" establishment service companies. The basis of organisation of the "higher" establishment companies will be a total of 151 of all ranks, including five officers, five warrant officers, eight sergeants, one trumpeter, and 132 other ranks; of the "lower" establishment companies, 83 of all ranks, including three officers, two warrant officers, seven sergeants, one trumpeter, and 70 other ranks.

Curragh, September 1922. As is already known by most people, the Curragh was finally evacuated by the British Forces on the 16th May, 1922, but the following may be of interest to numerous readers of the Corps Journal.

No doubt there were many who were glad to see the last of the Curragh, but there were also a very great number who looked back with sorrow on the great camp and its open surroundings. It was a dismal spot for the new arrival but those who were interested in outdoor sport and recreation soon grew to like the place, and it was a station which, in more peaceful times, would be hard to beat.

Ford Car, For Sale. — Late 1918, righthand Ford Touring Car, driven by owner and always maintained in excellent mechanical order. Fitted with patent carburettor and latest "Runbaken" commutator. Very complete equipment. Price £65. — Apply, c/o Editor.

Feltham. The first permanent depot of the R.A.S.C. without a horse on its establishment became an accomplished fact during the month of December, 1922, when No. 3, R.A.S.C. Depot, consisting of "R" (M.T.) Depot Company (the M.T. Driving School), the M.T. Repair Depot and the M.T. Stores Depot was formed. The formation of this depot is the outcome of the mechanicalization of the transport of the army, and, alas, one more nail in the coffin of the much lamented, dearly loved "Hairy," so rapidly becoming

extinct as far as the Corps is concerned. The site occupied by the depot is that of the old Aircraft acceptance park, built for the R.A.F. during 1917-19, but not actually completed until after the Armistice, and has been unoccupied since 1920. The depot is within half-a-mile of Feltham railway station on the L.S.W.R., 12 miles from London, and — as a landmark for visitors — two to three miles west of Twickenham football ground. The first detachment of the R.A.S.C. to occupy the depot was an advance party of "R" Depot Coy., under Capt. and Adjt H. M. Wright,

from Bulford, on 30th September, 1922. The headquarters of the depot followed on 20th November, and the remainder of "R" Coy. followed on the 15th December.

The transfer of M.T. Stores from Deptford commenced early in December, and should be completed by the end of March. The Repair Depot from Hounslow, it is hoped, will have moved in by the end of June.

The Hellespont Swum by R.A.S.C. Team. August 1923 Captain M. N. Dalton, Sergeant W. Allen, Corporal Johnson, Drivers Williams, Davies, and Marshall, and Private MacDonough, being the R.A.S.C. swimming team at Chanak, successfully swam the Hellespont on July 22nd from Sestos on the European shore to a point only about half a mile below Xerxes Mound, which is opposite Sestos on the Asiatic side. The team swam the distance in eighty minutes, and by zigzagging alternatively with and against the very powerful current, avoided being swept down to Kilid Bahr, four miles below, as has been the fate of previous swimmers.

(From the "Times," 31st July, 1933).

ABOVE: An informal outing by members of 12 Company in Tientsin,
1924. BELOW: The MT Store in Shanghai, 1924.

Lorry Subsidy, September 1923. It is officially announced that with a view to encouraging the use in commerce of a 30cwt. lorry, fitted with giant pneumatic tyres, the War Office will pay a subsidy of £40 a year to all purchasers of approved vehicles or chassis of British manufacture who enrol under the scheme which entitles the War Department to purchase such vehicles in national emergency at a price fixed by agreement at the date of enrolement.

Rank of Mechanical Transport Drivers, April 1925. In future the rank of private soldiers of the Mechanical Transport Section of the Corps, who are classified for tradesmen's rates of pay as "Drivers, internal combustion (lorry and car)" and "Drivers, steam (lorry and steam tractor)" will be described as "Driver·"

German Lorries on Manoeuvres. During Divisional Training of the B.A.O.R. it was decided that the baggage sections of each brigade should be composed of German hired vehicles.

A very varied assortment turned up at 28 Coy. a few days prior to the date on which they were required for duty, and the process of weeding out the "sheep" from the "goats" was carried out by Captain Galley, the Workshops Officer. It was no envious task to determine which were likely to "stay the course," for with the exception of three Thornycrofts, one F.W.D. and a few N.A.G.'s, which latter are undoubtedly the best lorries made in Germany, I doubt very much if a scrap heap would have been graced by their presence. Practically all the other German lorries had seen War Service as also had most of the drivers, the majority having been in the German M.T.

Football — Army Players Capped for England 1926. Lieut. K. Hegan and Sergt. F. Twine, who played so well for England against Ireland last November in the Amateur International Match, continue to add laurels to their fine football records. Both have been chosen for England against the Rest, on February 6th, Hegan this time transferring over from the right to his own wing. Twine remains at right back.

Hegan has gone even one better, having been selected to play in the English International — for the Rest against England. His present excellent form should bring him a cap before the season is over.

Voice from inside : "Step In!"

Plain Clothes, February 1928. Just before Christmas it was officially announced that the privilege of wearing plain clothes when off-duty (hitherto reserved for Officers, Warrant Officers and N.C.O.'s not below the rank of Sergeant), was to be extended to all N.C.O.s and men of good character when on furlough or pass, and also when "walking out" at their Station. The privilege is to be granted at the discretion of Commanding Officers, but we imagine the latter will seldom find cause for withholding it.

The Royal Army Service Corps Regimental Association Notes. During the past month great strides have been made and the

ABOVE: Morris 6 wheeler trials in Long Valley, Aldershot, 1926.
BELOW: Three-wheeled motor cycle, converted about 1923 by the
workshop in Buller Barracks. It was trialled but not developed further.

Association is now taking shape. We are pleased to hear that Branches are in course of formation at Aldershot, Feltham, Shorncliffe, Chatham, Colchester, York, Belfast, Edinburgh, Glasgow and Perth.

Mechanization, 1929. The programme of mechanization for 1929 became known some days after the publication of the Army Estimates. The gradual extinction of the H.T. Companies of the R.A.S.C. is to proceed, and two will meet their Waterloo in 1929.

The Mechanical Transport of the Corps in 1929 is to be two higher establishment Companies with their own workshops, and three without. Of lower establishment Companies there are to be ten with and five without workshops. There are also, of course, the Depot Company and the Depot Driving Company.

The Watch on the Rhine. The end of November will see the departure from Germany of 28, 29 and 34 (M.T.) Companies. A warm welcome awaits them at Aldershot and Catterick. Eleven years have passed since the British garrison was established on the Rhine. From all points of view, the withdrawal of troops is to be heartily welcomed.

Supplies by Aircraft, February 1931. The Army, Navy and Air Force Gazette, in a recent issue, contained a most interesting account of the supply of food to a column of troops on the march. The experiment was carried out on the North-West Frontier of India in September last with marked success.

The details show that the column, approximately 1,000 strong, started from Dargai for Chitral on September 5th, and as an experiment it was decided to ration them completely for two days from the air.

Arrived at their halting place, the column marked out a large circle on the ground in which the aircraft were to drop the rations. On the first day forty-eight of the fifty-six loads were successfully parachuted down, most of them falling within the circle of the dropping

area. On the second day — profiting no doubt by experience — fifty-four out of the fifty-six loads were successfully dropped at Chakdarra. The outcome was that the troops were fed for two days by the Royal Air Force, the first time in history that so large a military force had been completely rationed from the air. The parachute apparatus worked most successfully. It is designed so that it can take boxes, and any form of load can be used quite easily. The country was not easy for such a test, and the satisfactory outcome of the attempt indicates how, with efficient aircraft co-operation, the progress of armies may be accelerated.

Cut in Pay, October 1931. Not one of us likes to have his income reduced, and it is safe to say that every income is in process of reduction. His Majesty the King has set a magnificent example to the nation with his personal contribution of £50,000 to the country's exchequer in its hour of supreme peril. The Army, in common with all Departments of State, has been called upon to make heavy sacrifices. The general reduction of pay which takes effect from October 1st will be felt acutely by all ranks.

ABOVE: Corps Week Subalterns' Race 1931: participants are H. M. Gough, F. Newmarch, G. A. B. McLellan, W. O. Phillips, T. M. R. Briggs, W. G. Roe, A. B. Ilton, E. R. Goode, P. J. L. W. Lane, C. V. Ferrey, A. F. J. Elmslie, R. H. Daunt, F. K. Barnes, W. H. Western, C. B. Langdon, S. M. Griffiths, W. J. Crowe and J. Thompson. (B) BELOW: 25 Company group in front of a Handley Page HP 42 at Heliopolis Aerodrome, Cairo, February 1934.

Territorial Mechanization, October 1932. The War Office, pursuing its policy of mechanizing the Territorial Army, has issued an order to the T.A. Associations concerned, stating that it has been decided to mechanize the Divisional R.A.S.C. and Field Ambulance, R.A.M.C.

The order states that no contract for horses required by the present establishment for drills or for camps of Divisional Trains or Field Ambulances should be made by Territorial Army Associations.

Hore-Belisha, December 1932. We offer our congratulations to Major I. Hore-Belisha on his appointment as Financial Secretary to the Treasury. During the Great War, Major Hore-Belisha held a temporary commission in the Corps. Commissioned in September, 1914, he landed in France early in November and served with the 5th Divisional Train. Later he was attached to the Third Army Headquarters for temporary duty and then employed at G.H.Q. on the Supply Purchase Board. He also served in Salonika and was mentioned in despatches. He is the Liberal-National Member for Devonport.

Sandwiches for Soldiers, December 1932. Railway buffets will in future cater for soldiers newly returned from abroad on their journey from their port of arrival to their barracks. Up to now the soldiers have been sustained by what they bought. The War Office has now made arrangements with the railway companies by which the men will get meals at the station buffets in exchange for vouchers.

If the soldier will reach his home camp by 1 p.m he will have a 9d voucher entitling him to a luncheon consisting of a meat sandwich, a slice of cake, a round of bread and butter and a cup of tea or coffee. If he will be in barracks before 6 pm he gets a further voucher worth 6d with which he can obtain a similar meal without the cake. If he will be at his destination after 6 pm he will receive for the journey a 9d and three 6d vouchers. The 6d vouchers can be used for a 6d meal and 1s

meal, the latter consisting of two meat sandwiches, or one sandwich and one meat pie, and round of bread and butter, 1½oz of cheese, and a cup of tea or coffee. On a journey lasting until morning there will be a 9d breakfast voucher.

Meat pies are to be of an average weight of 4 oz, and the sandwich to be supplied must contain at least an ounce of meat.

Army School of Cookery, February 1933. Cooking and catering, like most other activities in the Army, have made considerable strides during the past few years, and rightly so, for no year should ever pass without some improvement being made. It is not always fully realized that the Royal Army Service Corps is entirely responsible for the training of officers, N.C.Os. and men of the Regular and Territorial Armies, and a limited number of senior N.C.Os. of the Royal Marines and Royal Air Force, in these two important subjects.

During the year 1932 no less than 650 N.C.Os. and men were trained at the School,

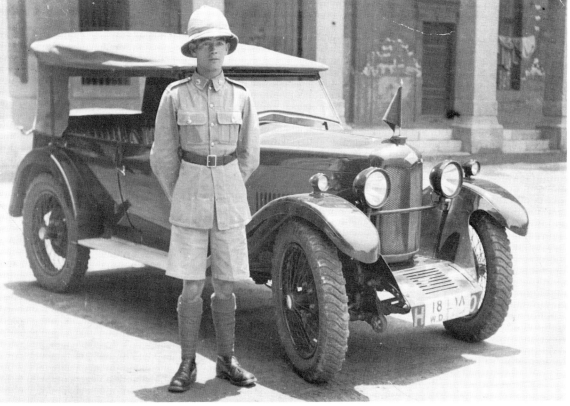

ABOVE: Veterans' Egg and Spoon Race, Corps Week 1931 — techniques
vary greatly. (B) BELOW: Driver H. J. Cullum and his Riley 9 staff car at
Kass el Nil Barracks, 1931.

and eleven courses were held for 126 officers. In order to offer every facility for instruction, extra accommodation had to be found, and War Office approval was obtained for the reappropriation of certain buildings which allow the School five additional lecture and demonstration rooms, and a museum. Thanks to the Royal Engineers and the Army Vocational Training Centre, the rooms are now unrecognizable as barrack rooms.

Tug-of-War, Feltham, August 1933. As stated earlier in our notes, our tug-of-war team has won the Army Championship at Olympia this year.

This is the first time this championship has been won by a Corps team, and it is hoped it will be the forerunner of more victories in the future.

We believe we are correct in saying that no other Corps team but Feltham has ever participated in this event.

Haifa, November 1933. Our Detachment has been dispersed over Northern Palestine with companies of the Seaforth Highlanders, and we are looking forward to concentration at Athlit for our Annual Training.

We think we have added to the various duties performed by the Corps, for we had the honour to provide a driver and hearse for the body of the late King Feisal of Iraq. Our one remaining lorry was converted into a hearse at sixteen hours' notice — a very creditable performance, thanks to the aid of the Pioneer Sergeant.

The coffin containing the body of the King was brought to Haifa by warship, the naval guard of honour acting as pall-bearers from the cruiser to the hearse. Lieut. Clarke, O.C. Detachment, was placed in charge of the funeral procession, which went from the docks to the landing-ground, six miles away, where an R.A.F. bomber was waiting to convey the coffin to Baghdad.

Labour Companies, May 1934. In the JOURNAL of March, 1934, we referred to the

fact that it was not generally known that the first Labour Company was an A.S.C. Unit.

The company consisted of stevedores and was very hurriedly thrown together in 1914 when it was decided to move our overseas base to St. Nazaire.

Catterick to Saar, February 1935. 51 Company may be the youngest of those at home, but it has shown us how well it can move, for in less than forty-eight hours after being placed under orders for important duty with the International Force in the Saar, the Company

Carry a tin of "SKIPPERS" in your Haversack

" Skippers " are so appetising. " Skippers " are so savoury. They make dry bread enjoyable, and are the tastiest, most delicious, "summat to your tea or supper" that you can find.

Get a tin of " Skippers " at your canteen and slip it in your pocket or haversack ; you will be glad of it as a " reserve" and will find " Skippers " very sustaining on a long day. The flat tin is so easy to carry and so easy to open.

Send us a postcard if your canteen does not stock them.

marched out of Catterick at 8.30 a.m. on 13th December, and arrived at Feltham at 6 p.m. the next day. In this short space of time, pesonnel had to be prepared, and regimental stores and equipment drawn from the Ordnance before the Company marched out complete in those respects, together with a proportion of the new establishment of vehicles.

The following day, the balance of vehicles was issued from the Vehicle Reception Depot, namely, 31 motor-cars, 21 lorries, 12 trailers,

ABOVE: Peace-keeping in Palestine in the 1930s: clearing the road block near Nablus. BELOW: 20 Company anti-gas training on 1938 manoeuvres. (G)

and 7 motor-cycles, while the Ordnance at Aldershot handed over 4 motor-cars and 8 kitchen trailers, together with the balance of stores and equipment to complete the special equipment of the Company for this particular duty abroad.

On Sunday morning, 16th December, 51 Company marched from Feltham to Shorncliffe with a total strength of 6 motor-cycles, 33 motor-cars, 24 lorries and 13 trailers. These vehicles were embarked on the 17th and arrived at Calais on the 18th. On the 19th they had reached Douai, Mezieres on the 20th, and Saarbrucken on the 21st — ten days after being ordered to the Saar.

From Shorncliffe, 46 Company accompanied 51 Company to the final destination. Those of the Corps at home may have already seen on the films the arrival of these companies, and will agree as to their smart appearance as a whole, and perhaps feel some pang of regret at not being with them in their new and interesting work, and thus gain first-hand knowledge of the value of the British soldier as a keeper of the peace in any part of the world.

The Corps at home and abroad wish their comrades in these two companies all the best of success and good luck, and think that in missing Christmas in England they will be amply rewarded by the experience gained. Well done, Catterick, Shorncliffe and Feltham, for each has done its fair share of getting a move on.

Exchange Wanted, April 1935. Lance-Corporal (Clerk), ordered Egypt in April desires exchange with individual not for overseas, or one who is under orders for Malta. Apply L./Cpl. G. Anders, c/o R.A.S.C. Office, Government House, Portsmouth.

Somaliland Watch, January 1936. "These are anxious days for Sir Arthur Lawrance, Governor of British Somaliland, and Colonel C. V. Bennett, commandant of the Camel Corps, watching, with a small garrison, the long and lonely frontier along which the Italian southern army is advancing towards Harar.

"Violation of the frontier has to be prevented, and British Somalis have to be dissuaded from stepping over the border to take part in the fighting.

"Colonel Bennett is the only Royal Army Service Corps officer now commanding a fighting unit. He was sent to Somaliland to carry out the partial mechanisation of the Camel Corps, and did his job so efficiently that he succeeded to the command of the troops there."

Bringing up Reinforcements

At the right moment, that is the time when real help is wanted. Bluebell is ready always to lend a hand when polishing is being done. It is a service polish which gives a brilliant finish at the right time.

brings brightness and brings it quickly

Cans: Petrol and Otherwise, February 1936. All officers who have attended a War Course at the R.A.S.C. Training Centre know that the production of sufficient cans for the storage and transport of the prodigious amount of petrol required in the opening stages of any campaign is a problem of major importance, for with the increase of road side pumps the petrol-can in civilian life has gradually become obsolete.

Air-Consciousness, September 1936. We read of experiments in camouflage, of officers and men going up to appraise the results of their efforts at concealment, of definite attacks on

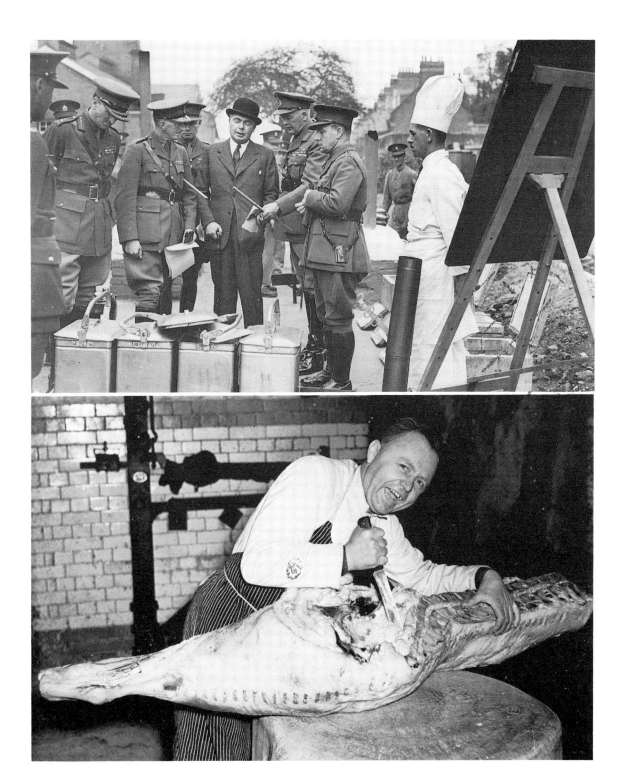

ABOVE: The War Minister, ex-Major Hore-Belisha ASC, visits the RASC
School of Cookery in Clayton Barracks, Aldershot, July 1937. BELOW:
Master Butcher WO2 Gow, clearly an enthusiast, May 1935.

convoys being arranged in co-operation with the R.A.F., of the extended use of air photography, and of practical demonstrations of decontamination.

Hose-Tops, October 1936. In consequence of A.C.I. 185/36 authorizing the provision of hose-tops and short puttees for wear by other ranks with khaki shorts at stations abroad on such occasions as the G.O.C.-in-C. may determine, a regimental pattern of hose-tops has been approved. These are obtainable from the N.A.A.F.I. at the stations in question at regulated prices.

These hose-tops incorporate the Corps colours; the stripes are of equal width, blue being at the top on the free-end as in the Corps flag.

Palace Duties, London District, February 1937. Extract from Adjutant's Detail, dated 5th December, 1936. — ". . . in addition to L./Cpl Pearce and L./Cpl Hunter-Rowe permanently employed as motor-cyclists to His Majesty at least 3 extra motor cyclists are to stand by for 'Palace Duties.' . . ."

At 11.30 p.m. on 9th December, 1936, a message was received at Kensington Barracks for two motor-cyclists to proceed to No. 10 Downing Street. (Two were required owing to the thick fog and the possibility of a casualty.)

Cpl Sheppey there took over a red-sealed despatch case carrying the abdication documents for signature by His Majesty King Edward VIII, and Cpl Sheppey and Dvr. Knapton set off on their fateful journey to Fort Belvedere.

The Coronation Year Cup Final, May 1937. Lieut. A. Campbell as O. i/c Football must receive his full share of these congratulations as well as L./Cpl. Gray, the captain, and every member of the team, all working under the general supervision of the Adjutant (Major Craig-McFeely), to whose care and inspiration it very largely owes its success.

Field Cooking, July 1937. We welcome the designation of the new Cooker, Portable, No.

1. which now officially replaces the Kitchen, Minor Formation. The latter phrase had always seemed an inadequate description, for no one quite knew what constituted a minor formation.

Dress, October 1937. Puttees are no longer to be worn by our drivers of mechanically propelled vehicles (including cycles) when they are driving such vehicles.

Football, February 1938. Our last issue was in the press before word came through of another spectacular success which must be added to the list of outstanding performances by the Corps in 1937. We refer to the Duke of Connaught Cup which was won by the Training Centre team, whom we congratulate most heartily. The cup is open for competition to the whole Army, in two series: (a) at home; and (b) abroad; and it is with so little sense of pride that every member of the Corps may realize that this trophy is now held for the first

ABOVE: The Dance Band in the Corps Theatre, Aldershot, 1927.
BELOW: A muddy moment during the 1938 Army Motor Cycle
Championships in Aldershot. (T)

time by an R.A.S.C. unit. Everybody knows that Major Booth is the inspiration of the team and to him and to all its members we repeat our congratulations on being the champion revolver team of the Army at home.

The match was instituted in 1893, but as the conditions for 1937 were somewhat altered from those for previous years no comparison can be made on the actual scores. The Training Centre team was third in the competition in 1936 with 277 out of 360 possible points, and won in 1937 with 526 out of 648.

Another individual success for 1937 remains to be accorded. Trumpet-Major Townsend, who was a member of the champion revolver team, has won the Revolver Cup which is in effect the Individual Pistol Championship of the Army at home. Again on behalf of the Corps we congratulate him most heartily on his title.

And so on this hitherto unattained height of achievement ends our records of Corps activities in coronation year.

Woolwich. Many of our older generation may learn with regret of the passing of the Riding School at Woolwich, and its conversion into M.T. workshops. The disappearance of the last of the horses from the station makes the retention of the School unnecessary, and it was considered that with the number of M.T. companies now in Woolwich, the old converted engine-sheds were no longer adequate for workshop requirements.

The Riding School itself has been turned into a fitters' and erecting shop with cement floor, capable of accommodating some seventeen vehicles. A corner has been partitioned off to form a technical store, and an up-to-date machine shop, with a complete equipment of modern machine tools, electrically driven, has been installed. The gallery has been extended and enclosed, and affords ample office accommodation.

Band. Foremost among the outstanding events which we have to record is the announcement made to the Corps by the

Secretary of State for War that in honour of the occasion, His Majesty The King has been pleased to approve the official recognition of our Corps Band.

Sadler, September 1938. Our cricket news in this issue records the highest score ever made by an individual in Corps cricket, a brilliant 183 by Sergt. L. A. J. Sadler, in the match against the Free Foresters. The honour had previously been held by Brigadier W. N. ("William") White, C.B., D.S.O., with 174, against the Royal Tank Corps in 1927.

That reminds me, have a

PLAYER

The Quality and Quantity Cigarette

Band, October 1938. The announcement by the Secretary of State for War on Jubilee Sunday has now been implemented by the appointment of Bandmaster A. Young. A.R.C.M., whom we welcome as the first official Bandmaster of the Corps Band. The peace establishment of the Band will be, in addition, 1 Band Sergeant, 1 Band Corporal, and 22 Bandsmen.

Dress. In case some doubt arises in the future as to when S.D. trousers (without turn-ups)

ABOVE: Visit of the Duke of Connaught to Buller Barracks in 1932,
accompanied by Lieut-Colonel E. H. Fitzherbert. (B) BELOW: Sergeants'
Mess New Year celebrations in the Corps Theatre; "Little Miss 1939"
arrived at midnight.

were introduced for the ceremonial dress of the Corps, we record it here that these were authorized for wear at home stations, and by the T.A. and S.R. in August, 1938.

Coffins. The reference in the Jubilee Journal to the use of old Chinese horizontal burial vaults for baking (with coffins as firewood) has prompted Capt. L. C. Bagg (ret. pay) to send us an extract from "Recollections of Forty Years' Service," by Major-General Sir A. B. Tulloch, K.C.B., C.M.G., published by Blackwoods in 1903, in which is related the further use of coffins by our ever-resourceful Commissariat bakers.

"The troops sent up to Peking in 1860 (after the Taku Forts incident) were returning to Tientsin. They had enough meat, but the men were becoming very tired of the biscuit. By great good luck we came on a large store of excellent flour at one village on the way down, but there was nothing in which our bakers could mix the dough, until I found a brand-new Chinese coffin in a carpenter's shop. The bakers were up all night, and next morning the Regiment had enough bread to last them to Tientsin. The tired bakers I put in the boats with the knapsacks."

Army Technical School (Boys) Jersey (C.I.). December 1938. The School has now opened and has, at present, 243 boys.

The boys and ten N.C.O.s arrived on 6th October by the s.s. *Lorina* after an extremely unpleasant crossing; but in a remarkably short time the greener-hued faces took on their normal colour. Those who saw the boat entering St. Helier Harbour must have felt relieved that they had solid ground beneath them.

Officers — First Appointment to the R.A.S.C. January 1939. We learn that it has been decided to reintroduce the grant of commissions direct into The Royal Army Service Corps to Gentlemen Cadets of the Royal Military College, and to officers of the Supplementary Reserve and Territorial Army who qualify at the R.M.C. final term

examination. With effect from the final term examination (July, 1939) inclusive, and until further notice, fifteen commissions in the R.A.S.C. will be available for Gentlemen Cadets of the R.M.C., and to qualified officers of the Supplementary Reserve and Territorial Army each half-year.

Tientsin, July 1939. An innovation to Tientsin is the introduction of traffic "humps." Though these have been in use in Peking for some time, we understand that this is their first appearance in Tientsin. They consist of raised ground to the extent of about ten inches off the

"Driver, does this—aw—animal kick?" "Lord bless ye, no, sir: she ain't got no more kick in her than 'arf-a-pint o' Canteen Bitter."

road level and are excellent solutions to curb the activities of the speed fiends! We imagine that these "humps" could quite usefully be introduced at home, but doubt if the present Minister of Transport would like to assume the prefix "Humpy" or "Humps" before his name!

49th (WR) Division R.A.S.C. Leeds was made "R.A.S.C. conscious" and in seventeen days we recruited some 1,100 men. Could we have found the necessary electricians we could have sent off the wire "Unit complete" the day before conscription was announced. Our peak day was when over 300 applied, and we actually had medically examined and attested 181 men.

ABOVE: Field Kitchen of the 51st (Highland) Division RASC at annual camp in Gailes, Troon, 1939. CQMS David Scotland wears 'blues' issued to the 1937 Coronation party but inadvertently never handed in. (H) BELOW: The Quartermaster General and others visit Boyce Barracks, Crookham to observe the reception of Militia Men, 15 July 1939.

THE SECOND WORLD WAR 1939-1945

Militia Training Battalion, September 1939. We are proud to be able to record that what was not more than an idea at the beginning of this year is now an accomplished fact; and it is perhaps fitting that these notes should open with an expression of welcome to the six-hundred-odd militiamen who are now comfortably installed at Boyce Barracks, Crookham, under the Command of Lieut.-Colonel H. R. Dobb, O.B.E., and are already well advanced in their training.

All Saints' Church, Ladysmith. We send a greeting to All Saints' Church, Ladysmith, on the occasion of the Jubilee of its Consecration, to be celebrated on 17th October, 1939.

This church has a long-standing connection with the Corps, for it contains a mural tablet in memory of Officers and Men of the Army Service Corps who lost their lives during the Siege of Ladysmith. For nearly forty years this tablet has been kept in good order, and these men's names have been honoured in the church.

We have been informed that a Thank-offering Jubilee Fund is being organized, to provide a belfry, the estimated cost being about £500.

We hope that all members of the Corps will join us in our message of greeting, and that many will send donations towards the fund to the Vicar, All Saints' Church, Ladysmith, Natal, South Africa.

Exchanges Wanted. Major due to proceed to Egypt, trooping season 1939/40, wishes to exchange with officer of similar rank. Reply to Box No. 137, c/o The Editor.

Sergt. (Clerk) desirous of exchanging with equivalent rank detailed for tour in Tientsin, Shanghai or Hong Kong. Reply to Box No. 138, c/o The Editor.

Regimental Association, October 1939. The work at Headquarters will continue as usual, but in the event of our being compelled to move our offices the new location will be notified to all concerned.

Shanghai. Unfortunately the present crisis is having its effect on the Detachment here. Our C.O. had to cut short his holiday in Japan and those of us who were going to Wei-Hei-Wei have had to unpack our suitcases and decide to enjoy the heat (and smells) of Shanghai instead of the sea-breezes of the North China Coast.

Tientsin. "Nil Sine Labore" has been amply brought before us in the past month. The Japanese blockade continues, the Hai Ho river is rising, the heat has daily become more

THIS 'NAZTI' WAR

THE OFFICER WHO LEFT HIS PRIVATE CAR IN THE M.T. YARD.

oppressive, nerves are on the edge and tempers have become frayed on many occasions but the R.A.S.C. duties have continued to function. We have now become the Carter Paterson, Woolworths, Marks & Spencers and C.W.S. for the military in this area. Apart from bringing in vegetables, etc., from Japanese controlled areas, we have been commissioned to transport milk (early morning deliveries at first, now nightly) meat, eggs, wood, sausages, and almost every issued R.A.S.C. commodity. In addition, transport arrangements for the conveyance of companies to and from the railway station on changes over from Peking and Shanhaikuan have been carried out without a hitch. To complete our activities under very trying conditions, we have just completed Annual Weapon Training instruction and A.G. Training, and Physical Efficiency Tests are also to be carried out in the near future.

The food situation has caused some concern, as the anti-British propaganda which has been bolstered to alarming heights has resulted in contractors defaulting.

ABOVE: Wartime recruits in Buller Barracks 1940: the Army was still using 1908 pattern webbing; Ross rifles were carried by the trainers. (G) BELOW: Bedford OYs are issued from No2 MT Depôt, Slough, during the winter of 1939-40. (G)

Presumably John Chinaman rightly considers that he would look much better with his head on than off, and this is seemingly the penalty for supplying foodstuffs to the offending "Yingoes." However, supplies have been maintained and we have neither begged, borrowed, nor stolen or even broken into reserves yet, which proves that there are ways of overcoming even the most stringent regulations. A local butchers' strike, coupled with the prevailing conditions, started speculation on the advantages or disadvantages of vegetarian diet. But again such debaters had reckoned without the Corps. Twenty-four hours after the strike had begun our Supply Depot Superintendent (of worthy proportions) successfully herded thirty head of extremely good looking cattle in to the Transport Yard Stables. Dame rumour suggested we were to be treated to a rodeo to relieve the tediousness of life, but we were pleased to see how false she was when Captain Grieve selected the fairest (and fattest) of them all for an introduction to our Mohammedan Butcher. Needless to say introductions were short and courteous and it was with a sigh of relief that we put away our "Hay" diets.

Off to the War, January 1940. It was raining on the morning of 15th October when we fell in outside Clayton Barracks. This may have helped to accelerate our departure, for within three minutes of "Markers" we were marching off. We wore our overcoats, carried a blanket in our valises, together with one change of washing, the whole being surmounted by neatly rolled anti-gas capes and groundsheets. We marched off to the Government Siding, with vocal appeals to "Roll out the barrel" and husky reminiscences of life "Down Mexico way," the whole under the baton or cane of the leading officer.

The Corps Band was waiting at the station, and gave us half an hour of much-appreciated selections. I thought rather wistfully of listening to the band on a sunny afternoon of Corps cricket or on one of those colder days when the Corps soccer team attracted large crowds to Buller Ground in an Army Cup classic. Brigadier Blunt kindly saw us off.

The War to Date. As these lines are being written, in mid-December, the war on land and in the air may be said definitely to have settled down to its comparatively uneventful winter tempo. But the fight at sea goes on, and activity in the war of words known as propaganda is still intense.

PRICES IN FRANCE

In order that there may be no misunderstanding regarding the prices of CIGARETTES & TOBACCOS in the Institutes conducted in France by the

Navy, Army & Air Force Institutes

attention is directed to the fact that such prices are Duty Free.

Army Technical School (Boys) Jersey. In spite of a somewhat hurried return to our island retreat, occasioned by a curtailment of our summer holiday, the even tenor of our existence goes on steadily, in spite of alarms and excursions in other parts.

BEF Heroic Stand, July 1940. The following story concerns the R.A.S.C. in Belgium

ABOVE: Workshop of 11 Corps Troops Petrol Company in Elsenham, Essex, 1941-42. (G) BELOW: Hurried loading of food supplies during the retreat in Libya, c1942; a US manufactured Dodge is on the left, a Ford on the right. (G)

during the recent evacuation of the B.E.F. from Dunkirk.

If appears that Capt Williams was ordered to go forward and demolish a bridge near Nieuport on the night of Tuesday, 28th May. The bridge offered passage to enemy tanks which at that time were forcing a way through to cut off the retreat of our forces. For some reason the demolition had been overlooked, and Capt. Williams was inclined to regard his job as one not easy to do, since, for all he knew, he would have to make his way to the objective through enemy forces which were presumed to have already advanced. He was surprised when he met no resistance, but the reason for this became obvious when the bridge was reached. Enemy tanks were making desperate efforts to cross, but were being successfully repulsed by an R.A.S.C. detachment. These latter had seen the danger some time before, but, although not front-line troops well trained in such work, had collected anti-tank guns and other weapons suitable to the occasion and then taken up a defensive position, letting the rest of our troops leave them there and continue the retreat. The R.A.S.C. men had no means of demolishing the bridge, but prevented the enemy from crossing and held him for no less than thirty-six hours of unbroken effort. Capt. Williams was able to demolish the bridge and retire. The R.A.S.C. men again did a very useful service by driving all survivors off in lorries.

Dunkirk, June 4. Dunkirk evacuation now completed; Mr. Churchill announces that 335,000 allied troops had been evacuated in 857 British and many French ships; our casualties had totalled some 30,000 only, but all our material of B.E.F., including over 1,000 guns, had been lost.

BEF Awards, October 1940. It is with justifiable pride that we draw attention to the list of awards for distinguished service in the field. With the intensification of bombardment from the air, and the

development of mechanized mobile warfare, the fighting area in military operations has ceased to be confined to the vicinity of a "front line," with the result that now, even more than in the Great War, L. of C. troops are exposed to all the hazards of actual combat.

Dealing with the evacuation from Dunkirk the author quotes a Cornish able-seaman as saying: "The bravest man I ever saw was an R.A.S.C. sergeant. Eight Heinkels bombed

"HERR ENGLANDERS, WE MEAN NO HARM!"

the fifty men under him who were wading ammunition to our boat. I saw several of them fall dead. The sergeant grabbed a Bren gun, stood his ground in the middle of the beach and blazed away at them. When they came back he did the same thing again and drove them off."

Lancastria, No. 1 M.T. Depot, January 1941. The last phase of this unit overseas was disastrous, but far from inglorious. It ended in a long swim — but before they left the ship the men of the unit manned ten of the eleven light machine guns on board, until the decks were at too steep an angle for the tripods to stand, and the water was waist-high. And this in spite of casualties and damage caused to the guns by bomb fragments.

When they did at last leave the ship the "Corporals' Choir" led them in singing "Roll out the barrel," while the ship sank amid a welter of bombs, oil and machine-gun fire from the air. Even then, we are told, Capt. George Parsons, a veteran of the Corps, raised a laugh from the soaking crew when he found a lifeboat and exclaimed "Just the job!" and that Capt. D. Abbott, in charge of the light

ABOVE: Tank recovery during fighting in North Africa; with shells exploding too close for comfort, the recovery crew take cover. (G)
BELOW: Transport moves down an escarpment road carrying supplies to the Libyan battle area, June 1942. (G)

machine guns, caused a roar when, before going overboard, he discarded all his clothes — even his beloved field boots — but kept his tin hat on!

Turn of Time and Tide. At home the Army grows apace, both in men and equipment, while round our shores the watch goes on unceasingly for the grey shapes, looming through the mist, that may one day herald the moment that our defending troops long for — a chance to teach the Nazis that Britain's soil is inviolable. In this they are supported by over a million Home Guard, resolute and steadfast men, ready to defend the countryside to the last. Throughout the Empire, too, troops are forming up in vast numbers, training and being equipped in the latest manner.

R.A.S.C. Comforts Fund, April 1941. The Aldershot Branch of the R.A.S.C. Comforts Fund is now situated at the Headquarters of No. 1 Training Brigade at Buller Barracks, Aldershot, for reception and dispatch of comforts for men of the Corps, such as gloves, mittens, helmets, scarves, books, games and sweets. Gifts may be addressed to R.A.S.C. Comforts Fund, Headquarters, No. 1 Training Brigade, R.A.S.C., Aldershot.

George Medal, July 1941. Cpl. A. G. Wisbey, R.A.S.C. — In the same raid, Cpl. Wisby organized a party to put out incendiary bombs. He was then placed in charge of a lorry and a squad to help the civil powers as a rescue squad. Although the task of reaching his destination was extremely hazardous, he got through with his party. He returned to his company headquarters and was detailed to go to another part of the town with a party. He reached his objective. He then took charge of a squad and worked ceaselessly throughout the night and the following morning in total disregard of his own danger. He eventually attached himself and his squad to an A.R.P. centre, where he worked on one partially demolished house, and freed a trapped woman and extricated her head husband. He extricated a further woman and her daughter

and the dead husband. As there were no further ambulances available, he removed the woman to hospital.

R.A.S.C. Feats in Desert. Lorries Regular as Trains. October 1941. Writing in the Daily Telegraph, Richard Capell says: "While the Western Desert fronts are quiet no one, perhaps, leads a more strenuous life than the drivers of The Royal Army Service Corps convoys who, day in, day out, carry huge masses of ammunition, petrol and food to the forward areas." "All who use the Sidi Barrani

road are familiar with the sight of R.A.S.C. ten-ton lorries, which are more regular than trains, but these also travel along distant desert tracks.

I know of one forward supply depot deep in one of Africa's dustiest regions. The journey there has to be made over sand which is like a dry quagmire, but these drivers do it regularly. Apart from the heat, dust, and jolts, the monotony of the job is trying. Furthermore, there is ever present the risk of low-flying and machine-gunning aircraft, which occasionally succeed in taking toll. All this represents a great test of endurance, but the men are tough. Thanks to them, troops in most forward positions receive bread and excellent refrigerated meat, which, after the long, torrid journey, arrives ice-hard."

Band Tours. Since the outbreak of war the Band in its various combinations has given hundreds of performances, mainly to R.A.S.C. units throughout the country. It has seldom been possible to arrange prolonged

ABOVE: Unit NAAFI truck, Tripoli, 1943, visiting 97 Company, with
Black and White whisky. RIGHT: Hitler wouldn't like Army issue tea!
BELOW: Tank recovery vehicles at Tel-el-Eissa, North Africa, 1943,
prepare for a three-way pull, with a tank transporter waiting. (G)

visits to individual units, owing to the numerous demands on the Band and the fact that it is pooled for garrison duties; but several tours lasting seven or eight days and covering as much ground as possible in selected areas have been carried out. During the past twelve months places and surrounding districts visited include Mansfield, Sheffield, Tonbridge, Bulford, Tidworth, York, Blackpool, Cambridge, Bournemouth, Bristol, Cheltenham, Dorset and the South Coast. The Band has played at church parades and ceremonial parades, and has arranged numerous troops' and public concerts and dances.

Export? January 1942. The fact that goods made of raw materials in short supply owing to war conditions are advertised in this Magazine should not be taken as an indication that they are necessarily available for export.

The Paper Situation. January 1942. Drastic rationing of paper supplies has forced us to adopt one of two courses: either a big cut in distribution or an equally severe reduction in the size of the JOURNAL. The latter alternative seemed the lesser evil and has been adopted. The current issue contains only half the normal number of pages, but about three-quarters of the normal amount of text. Typographical changes and various other expedients, including much unavoidable compression, have enabled us, at some sacrifice of appearance, to preserve the regular features of the JOURNAL.

R.E.M.E., July 1942. On 1st June, 1942, the newly formed Corps of Royal Electrical and Mechanical Engineers came into being in the United Kingdom. It will operate as soon as possible in overseas theatres of war.

Tobruk, October 1942. Good Work of R.A.S.C. Units During the Siege. When Tobruk was surrounded by the enemy in April, 1941, there were several R.A.S.C. companies in the garrison. Apart from M.T.

companies, mention should be made of the excellent work of the field bakery which supplied the garrison throughout the siege with freshly baked white bread, despite continuous dive-bombing and machine-gunning attacks. Much of this bread was made from captured Italian flour. There was also an Advanced Supply Depot which never failed to provide the traditional bully and

"I shave at speed!" this Tommy whoops; "Just like we cut off Musso's troops!"

for **EASY** makes it easy!

7½d INCLUDES PURCHASE TAX

★ Easy lather stays moist longer. ★ It keeps the beard soft till every single hair has been smoothly shaved. ★ The stick lasts longer, and so saves you money.

A *LEVER* PRODUCT

biscuits, with "M. & V." as an occasional treat. Little or no fresh food was obtainable; any fresh fruit, such as oranges, arrived in very limited quantities and went to the hospital.

Tripoli. General Montgomery's Tribute to the Work of the Corps. April 1943. We publish . . . General Montgomery's personal message to the Eighth Army after the capture of Tripoli. In the course of it he pays a generous and striking tribute to the outstanding part played by the Corps throughout the Battle of Egypt. "I would like to make special mention of our R.A.S.C. drivers; these men drive long distances by day and night for long periods; they always deliver the goods. The R.A.S.C.

ABOVE: A Jaffa lighter on a Diamond T tank transporter at Derna docks,
after a nine day journey over desert roads in North Africa, at times
strafed by German fighters, c1942. (G) BELOW: Hessian camouflage
over a 15 cwt vehicle, North Africa, 1942-43. (G)

has risen to great heights during the operations we have undertaken, and as a corps it deserves the grateful thanks of every soldier in the Army."

Home Guard, July 1943. Many curious eyes were turned on two columns of transport that rolled through the streets of London on the afternoon of Saturday, 26th June. Civilians stared, Service men gaped. What was this? An armoured car with twin machine guns manned, led the convoy, followed by a butcher's van, a baker's van and many types of lorries, of all shapes, sizes and colours, several hundred of them rolling along in best convoy style. Nos. 1 and 2 London Transport Columns, Home Guard, were "on exercise"!

A Bridge Nobody Wanted, October 1943. The R.A.S.C. drivers and convoy leaders of our 10-ton Macks get some curious loads. One 10-ton Mack unit has been carting a bridge around Tripoli for some weeks, but nobody wants it. It is a nice bit of work and will span a wadi or a bad crater, and was probably badly needed by someone somewhere when it was ordered. It's a bit heart-breaking to be left with an unwanted bridge on your hands after you've brought it many miles.

Some Unusual Loads. Chatting with them over a tin of M. & V. on the Zuara salt flats recently, 'Crusader' learned that their 10-ton Macks have carried submarine batteries and torpedoes, while their drivers recently captured some German parachutists. The parachutists, members of a so-called "suicide" squad, were not thinking of suicide at all when the R.A.S.C. Mack-drivers came on the scene. On the contrary, they were sitting meekly on the parapet of a bridge waiting to be picked up, fed and watered.

Lieut. Groom's most harrowing experience, apart from finding a whole convoy bogged up to the axles after a night of heavy rain, was getting torpedoes out of Alexandria docks. They loaded the torpedoes, two to a lorry, but found that the vehicles with load were too big

to pass through the dock gates. They tried to squeeze them through very slowly; but an inch to spare, with enough explosives to sink a battleship behind them, was too much for the drivers. This problem was solved by removing a bit of the dock wall and, as always, the convoy got safely through.

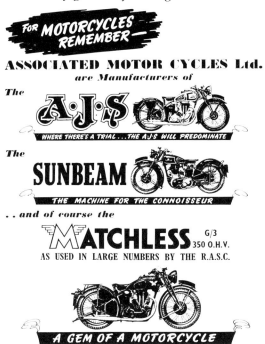

DUKWS. January 1944. The past year will be memorable in the history of the Corps for the first use of the Dukws, those astonishing engines of war which one of the most distinguished of administrative Generals has described as "the greatest thing of modern times for combined operation."

The honour of operating the amphibians in battle is prized by the R.A.S.C. The Dukws played a vital part in the invasion of Sicily and the Italian mainland.

Jerrican. Facts About the Army's New Petrol Container. The design of the "Jerrican," now in large-scale production in Great Britain, is essentially that of the German container captured in the Middle East. It appears to be the most serviceable and economical type for

LEFT: Bomb container MK 3 is packed for air dropping. RIGHT: Gas training with horses, Aldershot 1940. BELOW: Horse v bike: 'CSM Davis, a member of the 1938 Army International Motor Cycle Trials Team, had his eye on the camera so missed the gap in the brushwood left for him. He took a real purler . . . I went on and he stayed put with an immobilized bike and a broken finger'. (From album of Major Pearson.)

the arduous conditions of petrol supply in modern war.

The public has heard little either of the great achievements whereby the Royal Army Service Corps ensured that petroleum was never lacking in the fighting areas of Libya and North Africa, or of developments in the light of experience thus gained — developments which have proved their value in the Sicilian and Italian campaigns.

It was originally intended that the non-returnable four-gallon tins should be shipped abroad in wooden cases — two tins per case. But shortage of timber soon prevented this, and tins had to be carried naked or packed in cardboard cartons. Neither of these methods was ideal for sea transport, while on land some degree of leakage over rough going was inevitable. Nevertheless, the fact remains that these old-type tins provided the main source of the petrol supply that brought victory in North Africa. They are by no means entirely superseded now, for they still have many uses.

It's a Funny War. (From "Eighth Army News," dated 12th December, 1943). "It's a funny war," a German sergeant-major told a Canadian officer. "I'm going to Canada and you're going to Berlin." That's all there was to the conversation on the Adriatic beach, for the sergeant-major and a couple more of his fellow-prisoners of war saw a strange sight that made them rub their eyes.

They had heard of amphibious trucks, but hadn't seen them. So when a string of Dukws floated towards them, dropped their sea legs and waddled on to the beach with their ammunition, petrol and supplies they rubbed their eyes. Then a couple of Dukws which had emptied their precious loads pulled up, and took the prisoners away on the first leg of their journey to a prisoner-of-war cage. Most of them youngsters, they appeared to be in high spirits and a little thrilled by this new experience, like having a first ride on a roller coaster.

They pulled away just in time to hear the beginning of a terrific artillery shoot made possible by the amphibians. The Dukws, operated by the R.A.S.C., had been going day and night for five days. In the previous twenty-four hours they had taken forward some 700 tons of vital material, including 60,000 assorted rounds of artillery ammunition, 45,000 rations and 15,000 gallons of petrol. In addition they evacuated wounded prisoners of war.

Dukw "pilots" are R.A.S.C. drivers who have taken to the sea readily. Many of them worked through the Sicilian and Italian landings, and they are now developing traditions and habits of their own — like

AS DAY IS DAWNING

. . . And woe betide the careless clerk who goes more than seventeen paces.

giving the "thumbs up" or "V" sign when they take off or pass one another in the water, much in the same manner as pilots of the R.A.F. "I am where the ammunition is the thickest," joked a corporal from Lancashire, pointing to his load — three tons of high explosive on a Dukw.

Garigliano. R.A.S.C. Platoon Goes into the Line. During the first few days of the River Garigliano battle in Italy an R.A.S.C. platoon went into the line against a German counter-attack. Previously infantrymen and gunners had been horrified to see this platoon stacking its food, petrol and ammunition dumps ahead of the front line. One gunner officer was so thwarted in his role that he came up to complain that an ammunition dump had quite ruined his 6-pounder gun position by completely blocking his view of enemy-held ground.

LEFT: DUKW used for barge towing on the Chindwin, Burma, 1944. (G)
RIGHT: Some of the supplies for men in the Anzio bridgehead, May
1944. (G) BELOW: Passing-out parade of 246 Motor Boat Company.

Trials of Operating R.A.S.C. Water Transport. The minute which we print below was discovered in a very old War Office file in the writer's own handwriting:

"The stores enumerated at Folio 5A will be conveyed by W.D. vessele vesselle vessle vesle vesel, ship. — , Major-General."

Souvenirs, April 1944. Souvenir hunting became a major problem in the desert: It is incredible what men tried to send home. Middle East Orders made many sharp references to this problem and once stated that within a month more than five tons of equipment had been extracted from mails destined for home. Men tried to send machine guns, one piece at a time. Live 25-pdr. and 88-mm. shells were found in packages. German tin hats, football jerseys, complete uniforms, bayonets, food, cameras, binoculars, compasses, live hand grenades and detonators were among the more popular 'presents' that never left Egypt". From "I was an Eighth Army Driver" by RJ Crawford.

Supplies Behind the Scenes, July 1944. On 6th June, 1944, the Allied armies launched their attack on Hitler's Europe. Nearly three years had elapsed since the first plan for the supply and maintenance of these armies was discussed. The feeding of such armies is no last-minute affair. It demands hard thinking, exact planning and good guessing. Nor is it easy to guess. Forecasting is an art and not an exact science. To forecast accurately requires a deal of military knowledge and experience, and it is a matter of satisfaction to the officers of S.T.6 that the Army has never yet been short of food.

Airborne Bullocks, July 1944. West African troops, unloading transport aircraft on a forward landing strip in Burma recently, handled their strangest cargo — a consignment of bullocks.

Destined for transport duties in the Kaladan Valley campaign, the bullocks tested even the West African's capacity for rapid unloading.

Some "came quietly"; others, reluctant to leave their flying stable, dug in their heels. The combined efforts of a strong-arm squad of Gold Coasters finally unloaded the whole consignment safely.

One of the animals which staged a "lie-down strike" immediately on arrival, had its ambitions dashed when the unloading party picked it up bodily and restored it to the upright position. Within a few hours of landing, these bullocks, some fitted with specially designed pack saddles, others

'She won't go, Sarge. I think there's water in the petrol.'

between the shafts of country carts, were moving south to begin active service in the battle zone.

The light colour of some of the animals worried the camouflage experts for a while. The problem was overcome by dusting the more blonde of the bullocks with green dye. Wearing their new battle dress, this air-borne bullock company now forms a vital line in carrying essential stores and equipment to our forward troops in action against the Japanese.

Churchill, September 1944. When the Prime Minister during his recent visit to Normandy was due to be taken out to his ship an unforeseen delay occurred and the craft which was to take him was not available. A request was made to the R.A.S.C. motor-boat office and within three minutes an R.A.S.C. launch came alongside and performed the detail. The C.R.A.S.C. later received the following message: "The Prime Minister was grateful for the use of your boat this evening. He

ABOVE: Motor cycles await repair or disposal, Italy, 1944. BELOW:
Some really decent mud in the Netherlands: a Universal Carrier,
Humber Mk 111 Recce Car, Jeep and an M29 Weasel. (G)

remarked on the smart appearance and its good handling".

The Bailey Bridge, September 1944. One R.A.S.C. general transport company has a distinguished record of Bailey bridges to its credit from the invasion of Sicily onwards. The first operation in which vehicles were engaged was the restitution of the bridge which held up the entry of the fighting troops into Randazzo. It was a small bridge requiring only six vehicles under a corporal, but owing to its awkward situation and to the proximity of the enemy it was found impracticable to build it. It was decided, therefore, to build instead a diversion requiring engineer stores. The vehicles were unloaded and dispatched for the necessary stores and on their return the diversion was completed under heavy enemy fire, thus enabling the British forces to enter the town and clear it of the enemy. The corporal in command of the vehicles was awarded the Military Medal for his part in the operations.

Prisoners of War Fund. R.A.S.C. Regimental Association. It has been decided to open a special fund on behalf of R.A.S.C. prisoners of war. During the past twelve months there have been considerable developments with regard to our arrangements for the welfare of our comrades who have the misfortune to fall into the enemy's hands.

The R.A.S.C. at Arnhem, November 1944. The experiences of the men inside the Arnhem bridgehead have already been described often enough with both accuracy and detail, and the R.A.S.C. bore their full share. For the first day or two, before enemy reaction became severe, normal R.A.S.C. activities were carried on. A Divisional Maintenance Area was formed; the supplies landed in Hamilcar gliders were successfully cleared, although under spasmodic enemy fire; a fair proportion of the earlier supply drops were collected, and issues were made to units. Soon, however, the dumps came under heavy attention not only from the ubiquitous

mortars, but from small-arms and machine-gun fire, so that it became a matter of difficulty and danger to make further issues. The dumps were then moved into a position of greater safety and better concealment behind Divisional Headquarters. The enemy, however, seemed to be in no doubt as to their whereabouts, and the area was subjected to ever-increasing and extremely accurate mortar and shell fire.

On the fifth day, gaps in the defended perimeter became so wide and so dangerous that an R.A.S.C. force some seventy strong was ordered to take over a defence sector

during the night. they took up their position, and not only held it in the face of considerable attacks by infantry, tanks, S.P. guns, mortars and all the rest, but even succeeded in advancing one street. This was considered to be rather foolish, as it produced an unusually hefty counter-attack the following day. Nevertheless, the line was held; most of the R.A.S.C. force seem to have accounted for at least one German each, and when the order was given to retire the withdrawal was made in good order and the force was safely

ABOVE: A mule is loaded into a Dakota as part of 5th Indian Division's
support from Arakan for the besieged Imphal, Burma, 1944. (G) BELOW:
Mulberry Harbour in action in Normandy, 1944. (G)

evacuated across the river. The detachment gave as good an account of themselves as the peerless infantry fighting on each side of them.

Driver Becomes Paramount Chief. Three times in the past few years the people of the Lunia Chiefdom in the Bo district of Sierra Leone have tried to elect a Paramount Chief to succeed Paramount Chief Kata, who died over five years ago. Each time a deadlock was reached between the different candidates. Now at last Alfred Goro has succeeded in bridging the gap. He was unanimously chosen by the tribal authority to be their Paramount Chief. Alfred Goro is a serving soldier — a driver in the West African Army Service Corps, where he is known under the name of Alfred Scott. All will wish him every success in his new responsibilities.

Dvr Alfred Scott referred to above was granted leave to attend the election of a Paramount Chief. He was elected Chief and notified his Company Comander accordingly. He was instructed to return to his unit to be officially discharged from the Service and to be interviewed by the Area Commander. It is of interest to note the difference in status between a mere driver in the W.A.A.S.C. and a Paramount Chief as indicated by the telegram he sent to his Company Commander:

"To O.C. — Company

"From — Paramount Chief. Alfred Goro

"Inform Area Commander send lorry Tuesday Water Street accommodation required thirty followers."

Letter to the Editor. Dear Sir, In the September edition of the Corps Journal I read that you were publishing in the next edition an article on the arrival of the first British troops in Paris, which was a supply column carrying supplies for Paris. Although your heading, "R.A.S.C. Drivers were First British Troops in Paris," was correct, the actual first troops were R.A.S.C. drivers of this Company.

An Infantry Brigade Company, R.A.S.C.
British Liberation Army.

The Supply line in Burma, March 1945. "Along this road every day will flow, must flow, the food for the great army up forward. Do you realize that it is the largest single army in the world? For besides the British up there are Indian soldiers, Gurkhas, Americans, West Africans and East Africans, Chinese, Burmese and the warrior hill tribes of the jungle, the Nagas, the Chins, Kachins, Karens — altogether 600,000 troops are fighting in the Fourteenth Army, and all must eat. So every twenty-four hours 2,000 tons of food will go

Tokyo Next Stop

up that single-track mountain railway, and along those military roads. Motor trucks, jeeps, ox wagons, mules, donkeys and elephants will carry it up to the front. Though landslides block the railway or the highway and floods have swept away the bridges, supplies will get there."

The first "ducks" to take to the Irrawaddy River were those of an R.A.S.C. company which has been in India since 1942. Starting off as a G.T. company it changed over to "ducks" in October of last year. Its first

114

ABOVE: Jerricans are filled from bulk fuel tankers by a labour unit, North-West Europe, 1944. (G) BELOW: A pack mule team, used for supply in the mountains of Italy, threads its way through Adrano, 1944. (G)

important job in its new role was the towing into position of the 1,000-foot-long Bailey bridge spanning the Chindwin at Kalewa.

Buller Mess Celebrates the Half-Century. On 30th January, 1945, fifty years to the day after the celebration of the opening of buller Mess, fifty officers stationed at Aldershot and a number of guests sat down to dinner in honour of the Jubilee. The Corps band in the hall played selections from the programme of music played on that night fifty years ago.

Demobilization. Release Group No. 1. By Major P. K. Haworth, M.C. July 1945. It was easy to spot other parties on their way to be "demobbed." They all seemed remarkably decrepit; but as the combined ages of my own party of six totalled 316 years we may have looked a little bit part-worn ourselves. Taunton was our Mecca, ready to carry us off to our collecting unit — a hutted camp only a few minutes' drive away. Here we parted company with two N.C.Os. and a private who had travelled up from Aldershot with us. Lingering handshakes and last salutes as we dragged our cases and ourselves off to the Officers' Mess, where for an entrance fee of sixpence we were entitled to buy lunch and liquor.

At the dispersal centre an N.C.O. at the information bureau had the train timings at his finger-tips and advised us to stay the night. "Means an extra day's pay, too," he added. Space will not permit details of our last evening in the Army — perhaps it is just as well. After breakfast the next day — and a thoroughly hearty breakfast it was, too — we passed through "documentation" — all very efficient; only took ten minutes before were were whipped away to the clothing stores, where a super shop-walker measured each soldier for every possible purpose. His considered summing up of me was.

"Forty" — my chest measurement "Portly" and "Short".

In due course, believe it or not, I was led to an alcove in the clothing stores surmounted by that self-same slogan, and anyone who

passed could look in at me and glance at the words above the door and see "Forty, Portly Short." Sports coats for the "portly" are just a little on the flamboyant side perhaps, and in the end I chose a dark grey pin stripe which, considering the above mentioned

"RUSSIANS? All I said was ' I've got the RATIONS wiv me ' "

eccentricities of my figure, fitted me tolerably well. I toyed for a few moments with a trilby (pork-pie, green), but finally chose a sombre brown hat and some shoes and a first-rate mackintosh. All this was packed up in a neat

" Turn to the right where it says ' OUT OF BOUNDS,' then down the road marked ' NO ENTRY,' till you come to a bridge what's blown up. Then cross over where it says ' BEWARE OF MINES ' till you reach a sign marked ' UNEXPLODED BOMB '—and you're there. You can't miss it ! "

cardboard container so there was no need for me and my sparring partner, Freddie, to have lugged a couple of suitcases with us. In fact, all the arrangements went without a hitch.

The train was very crowded on the way back, and these are two of the remarks that reached me in the corridor from a carriage packed with men just released: "They must have known about my pension, mate. They tried to kill me with kindness." "They call this a release book and now I've got to go back to the wife."

ABOVE: A Weasel crosses flooded fields in the Netherlands during the winter of 1944-45, carrying wounded men. (G) BELOW: A Diamond T of 452 Company with Landing Craft for the crossing of the Rhine. (G)

Corps Week, July 1945. In this troublesome year of 1946 an attempt has been made to re-create the annual Corps Week, after a lapse of six years. It was not an easy task because only a few individuals had the experience of pre-war Corps Weeks and also much of the old data and accounts had been disposed of when the call for waste paper, etc., was made during the war. The theme adopted for this austerity year was the reunion of the Corps "family" (past, present and future) and was designed to cover all theatres in the world where the R.A.S.C. are serving, living or have operated.

R.I.A.S.C. Welcome, August 1945. In accordance with agreements between the War Office and India, some fifty Regular British officers in the Royal Indian Army Service Corps of various ranks whose careers in the Indian Army are being cut short owing the Indianization, are being transferred to the R.I.A.S.C. These officers will join the Corps with rank and precedence in accordance with their length of service.

Flag bombshell. September 1945. What a couple of months! The atomic bomb . . . Japan gives in . . . A new, or rather an adapted, Regimental March receives provisional approval and an alteration to the Corps Flag is proposed.

Letter to the Editor. November 1945. H.Q., Ceylon Army Command, S.E.A.C.
Dear Editor,

I do not think one could find a better example of *esprit de corps* than I came across the other day when I visited sick R.A.S.C. prisoners of war who had been flown direct from Singapore to Ceylon. I had taken some cap badges and numerals along with me in case I might be asked for them. Every man made this request except one, and when I asked him if he required one he pointed to his locker, where he had put his badge immediately on arrival. He said he had carefully retained it all through captivity and, though there had been many chances of

exchanging it for food or comforts, he was determined to wear his Corps badge when he came back.

Yours, etc.,
M. F. Farquharson-Roberts, Brigadier

Pluto, November 1946. The "Hais" high-pressure submarine pipe-lines, laid in the late summer of 1944 across the English Channel as part of operation "Pluto," are now being raised from the sea bed.

[*Reprinted by kind permission of the Editor of the " Star"*]
"Room 'shun, Orderly Officer! . . ."

Japan. Two platoons of 8 Company are now operating very busily in Tokyo with transport of all descriptions, but in between their duties they manage to compete as successfully as ever with the Russians at football. Some 400 miles away is the remainder of the unit, which in turn is well dispersed throughout the divisional area, the main body and headquarters being still housed by the seaside.

Batperson. It is strange how the idea persists among other ranks in the Army that the Colonel's wife lives in luxurious ease; despite the rigours of war and the desperate shortage of servants. A Colonel recently sent a man

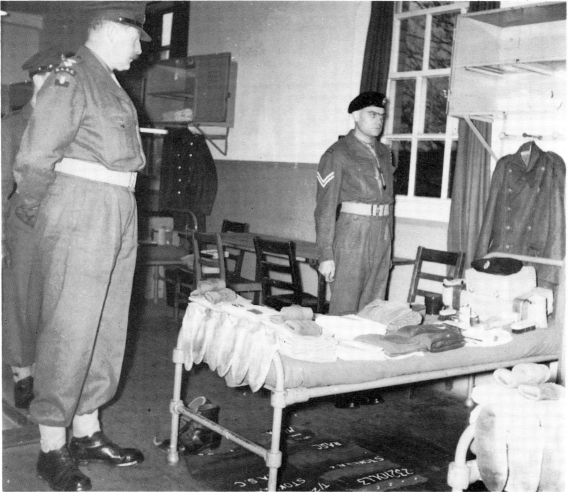

ABOVE: Buller Barracks Officers' Mess, Aldershot, April 1950. (I)
BELOW: Lieutenant Colonel 'Oliver' Cromwell inspects the kit of Cpl K.
Stokes, Depôt Battalion, Bordon, c1954.

round to his home to fetch some papers. The Colonel's wife, in the middle of her morning's dusting, answered the door in person and helped the man to find the documents. As he turned to go the soldier asked, "What's the old blighter like to work for?"

Berlin, The End of The Road, January 1947. To most of us during the war Berlin signified "the end of the road" without in any way detracting from the campaign against the Japanese. Certainly to all who served in 21 Army Group the occupation of Berlin by the Allies in the summer of 1945 was the end of the road. The R.A.S.C. were, of course, there to fulfil our normal supply and transport functions. In the early days of the summer of 1945 the British sector of Berlin was maintained by road along the great autobahn from Hanover to the Berlin suburb of Spandau.

Op "Woodpecker", April 1947. Germany abounds in dense forests scarcely touched by war, the home of wild boar and deer. It is to Germany, then, that we have turned to provide the timber to rebuild British homes destroyed by the German airmen. This task assumes the proportions of a major operation and the scheme for providing the timber has been appropriately named Operation "Woodpecker." Already the forests and woods of "Das wunderschöne Land" ring with the axe and loads of vital timber have begun their journey to the coast *en route* for Great Britain. The scheme is a combined operation by the North German Timber Control working in close co-operation with the Army of Occupation and the Control Commission for Germany.

The New Vehicle Sign, May 1947. Many of us will regret the passing of the red and green vehicle sign, but it is felt that the new blue and yellow sign, which is more distinctive, will enable a R.A.S.C. vehicle to be discerned more easily as such. The change-over has taken place so rapidly during the past few weeks that it is now becoming rare to see a W.D. vehicle bearing the old familiar colours on its mudguard and tail-board.

R.A.S.C. Museum, March 1948. It is impossible in a short article to do other than state a few facts and aspirations regarding our Museum. It was started in early 1945, having been in the minds of many Corps officers for several years prior to that, as being desirable.

Palestine: the Last Days, June 1948. By the time these notes appear the mandate in

Sketch by Capt. G. D. Machin, D.F.C., R.A.S.C.
THE COMPLIMENTS OF THE SEASON

Palestine will have ended and the last British troops will be awaiting their final orders to leave before 1st August. Thus closes a chapter of history which has shown the British soldier at his best in an atmosphere of political strife and bloodshed. In common with other Arms the Corps has borne its share of the brunt of these events, and it has proved to be no small share.

Army Sweet Ration, August 1948. Mr. Hollis asked the Secretary of State for War whether, in view of the monotony of sweets at the N.A.A.F.I., members of His Majesty's Forces will be allowed to draw their sweet rations from public shops.

Mr. Shinwell stated, in reply, that arrangements have been made for officers and other ranks on the lodging list to buy their sweet ration, if they wish, from ordinary shops. It would not, however, be practicable for troops generally to do this. In any case, he did not accept the suggestion made in the first part of the question.

ABOVE: The Queen's Baggage Section of 20 Company in Regents Park
Barracks, 1954: Standard Vanguard, Ford Thames and Commer 3 ton. (J)
BELOW: Boys' Company, Mandora Barracks, Aldershot, 1951.

Berlin, October 1948. 950 Company, R.A.S.C. (G.T.) (Berlin), are still very heavily involved in Operation "Plainfare." Approximately forty vehicles have been providing a twenty-four-hour service at Gatow for two months and the gradual relief by civilian-driven vehicles now taking place will be greatly appreciated.

Op Iceboat, 2nd Division. No doubt many of our readers are aware that the currency in the Western zones of Germany has recently been changed, but it is doubtful if they realize the part the Corps was called upon to play in this transaction. Operation "Iceboat," as it is called, meant much hard work for all the 2nd Divisional M.T. companies. In view of the valuable nature of the load only British-driver vehicles could be used, and in consquence every available M.T. company was called upon. The operation was extremely secret, and the vehicles had to rendezvous without any idea of the task in front of them.

Nazi Treasure. Once agin the R.A.S.C. have carried out an unusual task. For a considerable period 10 Company, R.A.S.C. vehicles have been employed in returning art treasures stolen or looted by the Nazis from all over Europe.

Army's Far East Fleet, February 1949. Assisting British Land Forces and Police in Malaya against Communist-inspired terrorism is a fleet of small craft of 986 R.A.S.C. Water Transport Company. Based on the Island of Pulo Brani opposite the dockland of Singapore South, this unit possesses craft ranging from several hundred tons, Tank Landing Ships and L.C.Ts., to a tiny four-seater motor-boat. Harbour launches, so unattractive to the eye and covered in by ugly grey awnings, are the cargo carriers of the little fleet. They carry the rations and supplies for two island garrisons and also play the part of ferry.

Service Dress — Officers, April 1949. The Secretary of State for War, Mr. Shinwell,

stated in reply to a question that Service dress is obsolescent except for officers of the rank of Colonel and above, and officers of horsed units. For the latter, Service dress is the normal dress for mounted parades. Colonels and above are allowed to wear Service dress on occasions when not on parade with troops wearing other types of uniform. No other officers are now allowed to buy Service dress, but those who still have it may wear it on various occasions.

"Now then, Gentlemen, a word about dress...."

Air Despatch, 799 Company, R.A.S.C. November 1949. Since 1944, when the Company was first formed from the permanent staff of No. 8 Training Battalion, it has provided crews for air-dropping at Arnhem, Burma, Netherlands, East Indies, Malaya and Hong Kong. We are now located in Singapore with air crews operating from Changi airfield and a detachment in Kuala Lumpur. One air crew is stationed in Hong Kong for training duties, and in the recent *Amethyst* incident on the Yangtse, two of this crew were on the Sunderland which took medical supplies to the ship.

Albert Hall Rally, January 1950. First Rally of the Royal Army Service Corps Association at the Royal Albert Hall, on 19th November, 1949. THe Corps Band, under its very capable musical director, Lieut F. J. Dean, was playing a varied programme of light music while the hall rapidly filled. Tier upon tier of expectant faces formed a congenial background to the arena, and on all sides, across vast spaces and

ABOVE: BAOR exercise scene, 7 Armoured Division, 1950s: Austin Champ, Ferret, BSA motor cycle and Bedford RL. (G) BELOW: Beaver of 130 Flight over Singapore City.

in the corridors were heard cries of pleasure and seen waving programmes as recognition became the prelude to reminiscence. It was not difficult to read the dumb-show signs which clearly said, "Come and have a quick one in the interval!"

Farewell, Connaught Barracks, Woolwich, April 1950. The time has come for the R.A.S.C. to hand over Connaught Barracks at Woolwich, and, except for small representation, to leave Woolwich Garrison. Thus another page of Corps history has been turned.

Luncheon Club, June 1950. The newly formed R.A.S.C. Officers' Luncheon Club held its first meeting at the Victory Club on 25th April. Approximately eighty officers sat down to lunch, the guest of honour being Lieut.-General Sir Humfrey Gale, who is President of the Club.

Livery for Mess Servants in Headquarter Mess. November 1952. It is very difficult and expensive to produce proper pre-war livery for the Mess servants of Headquarter Mess. It is, however, most desirable that these servants should be properly dressed and reflect in every way the tradition and dignity of the Headquarter Mess of the R.A.S.C.

With this in mind, it is considered that officers' pre-war Mess dress is capable of being altered and made into a very suitable livery. Will any officer who has reached the rank of substantive full Colonel please therefore consider presenting his old Mess dress to the Headquarter Mess for this purpose. All such presentations will be most gratefully acknowledged by the P.M.C.

North Malaya. 29 Company has had an unusual job. On 21st August the High Commissioner, General Sir Gerald Templer, told the inhabitants of Permatang Tinggi that unless they supplied information about the murder of a Resettlement Officer by 0900 hrs., 25th August, they would be sent to a detention camp. At 0840 hrs., 25 August, a convoy of the Company's vehicles arrived at Permatang Tinggi with the Officer Commanding, Police District. At 0900 hrs. the first vehicle was loaded with families and at 1300 hrs. the villagers were in the detention camp at Ipoh, some 100 miles away.

Coronation. For some time now No 1 Training Battalion has been very actively engaged in preparations for the Coronation, and troops are to be seen marching long distances in practising for route-lining duties. The Horse Transport Training Company, besides preparing for its usual circus activities for shows, etc., is also training a number of horses for Coronation duties. Capt. Boon

The Driver who thought the Daily Task was a newspaper.

practically lives in the Royal Mews when he is not touring the country inspecting and reconditioning a number of landaus, which will be used in the procession. A number of other officers have been detailed for various Coronation duties.

Mount Everest Expedition, July 1953. It will be of interest to readers to know that the rations used by the British Mount Everest Expedition were supplied by the R.A.S.C. except for certain special commodities. The main ration pack was a modified form of the ten-men composite ration and the assault ration pack was based essentially on the experimental British twenty-four-hour snow ration.

R.M.A. Sandhurst. Since the war it has been customary each year to give a number of demonstrations at Buller Barracks of the work

An Alvis Stalwart of 2 Company in Aden; the dhow sign is of Aden Brigade.

of the Corps, and among the most successful have been those given to cadets of the Royal Military Academy Sandhurst. However, this year we were faced with a choice; either the demonstration had to be abandoned, or it had to take place at Sandhurst. It was, of course, no choice at all — in spite of the misgivings of those called upon to arrange this transference of the mountain to Mahomet. Since this is the first time the Corps has carried out the demonstration inside these famous grounds, it is felt that others, in addition to the 220 all ranks who took part, may be interested in the event.

Most of the demonstration took place in the area between Old College and the lake, a magnificent setting, to which glorious weather did full justice on the day. The programme was divided into three parts; a demonstration of a transport platoon on the move, a number of static stands covering the major activities of the Corps, and, as tail-piece, a display by the Horse Transport Training Company.

Tanker Strike, December 1953. To help with the petrol deliveries in London during the recent strike, 19 and 53 Companies (North Midland District) between them sent 170 all ranks for Operation "Tanker." They have now returned having enjoyed their unusual role, in which they were kept extremely busy. Interesting tales are circulating about the help the military received from the strikers — in some instances even instructing our drivers in the best way of getting into and out of awkward delivery points.

5 Training Battalion, January 1955. Last month the hundred-thousandth National Serviceman passed through this Battalion. He is No. 23088420 Pte. T. Willbourn.

Great War Song, May 1955. Mr. Edward C. H. Rowland, who wrote the 1914-18 song "Mademoiselle from Armentieres," died at his home in Avenue Road, Belmont, Sutton, Surrey, during the week-end after a short illness. He was 72.

The song that became one of the favourites of the British troops was written in a few minutes by Mr Rowland, then a sergeant of the Royal Army Service Corps. He scribbled it on the back of an envelope in an Armentieres cafe in March, 1915. Something catchy was wanted for a troop show that night. The cafe waitress inspired the title. The song was set to music immediately afterwards by a friend, Lieut. Gitz-Rice, a Canadian composer, who has since died.

SPEND YOUR HOLIDAYS AT R.A.S.C. Hotels

Kenya, January 1956. In the campaign against the Mau Mau terrorists in Kenya, which is being fought by British and African troops over terrain varying between mountain, moorland and dense forest, criss-crossed by precipitous gorges and tortuous rivers, ponies and mules have come into their own. Operating up to heights of 12,000 and 14,000 feet, they carry rations, water, ammunition and weapons. This vital supply role is being carried out by 67 (Animal Transport) Company, East African Army Service Corps, from its base at Nanyuki.

British Commonwealth Forces Korea, March 1956. It is only those few of the Corps with experience of a winter in Korea who have any conception of how cold it is. The rivers and countryside consisting of paddy fields are frozen hard, the roads are sheets of glass and everyone is very cold. Once the bread leaves the bakery, it is soon frozen solid. Movement out of doors is limited to necessity, particularly when the wind is from the west — Siberia.

ABOVE: Bedford RLs in troop-carrying role, Malaya, 1960s. BELOW:
RCT Formation Parade on 'W' Square, Buller Barracks, 15 July 1965.
Lieutenant-General Sir James Cassels is accompanied by Major-General
Errol Londsdale. (The author handed out badges, hidden away in the
rear rank). (K)

5 Training Battalion, October 1956. Since the Suez Canal emergency arose at the beginning of the month, Blenheim has been responsible for the reception of over 3,500 men recalled from the reserve. The Battalion has received very welcome cooperation from the other training battalions, and also from the R.A.P.C., for which it is very grateful.

Boxing, April 1957. The brilliant progress of the 15 Training Battalion boxing team through the eliminating contests in U.K. to win in B.A.O.R. the Army Final against the 1st Bn., The King's Regiment (Liverpool) has been watched with interest by all members of the Corps. Well done, 15 Battalion! Your boxing skill, fitness and determination to win have been rewarded.

Junior Leaders. On 27th February all boys' units became junior leaders' units. The change in title does not indicate so much a change in the aims of the units as a recognition of their role, a role which is not always fully appreciated by the public — or even by members of the services. Our junior leaders are all long-term Regulars who have enlisted for nine years with the colours, and it is hoped will be the senior N.C.Os. and warrant officers of the future.

Central Malaya, 55 Company (Air Despatch). November 1957. We regret to say that the three R.A.F. crew of the plane were all killed in the crash, yet none of the despatchers was seriously injured; and before the crashed plane was located by searching aircraft two of the despatchers had started to walk the twenty-odd miles to the nearest main road in order to obtain help.

Once the crash was located, parachutists, including doctors, went in, and a small party of the 22 S.A.S. Regiment went on foot to meet the two despatchers who were on their way out of the jungle. They met after a short while and the party then proceeded to the scene of the crash for evacuation by helicopter. We are pleased to report that they are all fully recovered from their ordeal.

7 Armoured Division, January 1958. 109 Squadron (A.P.C.) — 109 Squadron has now disbanded, having carried out its armoured personnel carrier role in this Division for a year and a half, under command of 1st Bn. The Devonshire Regiment. During a farewell visit from the Divisional Commander, Major-General J. W. Hackett, addressed the Squadron on parade and expressed his gratitude for the work it had done in the Division. Now we have handed over our Saracens to "C" Squadron 14th/20th The King's Hussars, and have been able to help them by providing officer and N.C.O.

A STOUT LORRY

is the Albion 30 M.P.H. 5/6½ tonner

Sturdiness of construction, unequalled length of life, freedom from breakdown, and outstanding economy of operation are the qualities which justify the popularity of the range of 5 and 6½-tons Albion petrol engined chassis.

With normal bodywork the unladen weight of a platform lorry can be kept under 3-tons—legal speed 30 m.p.h. Also available is the "Chieftain" range of 5-6½ ton chassis with Albion oil engine.

Albion
MOTORS LIMITED
SCOTSTOUN GLASGOW W.4.
2 LYGON PLACE, EBURY ST., LONDON VICTORIA, S.W.1

instructors to teach them to handle these complicated vehicles.

Arabian Peninsula, November 1958. 90 Company, which has been forming since January, may now be regarded as a going concern. The basis of the company was 16 Independent Transport Platoon which Capt. Murphy brought over from Aqaba. To this have come reinforcements from U.K., Cyprus and, mainly, Tripolitania.

The work of the Company is proving most varied — from the towing of 25-pounders on

Driver Bath and LCpl Brewer pack live chickens for air dropping to
Gurkhas on operations in the Borneo jungle: 55 Air Despatch Company
in Kuching, 1966.

ceremonial parades to the most gruelling of journeys on convoys up-country — and the carrying of V.I.P.s. As the only permanent M.T. Company in the Colony, it is not surprising that we are regarded as Jacks-of-all-trades where transport is concerned.

Pipe Bands in Unique "Retreat" Event, July 1959. The three pipe bands of the Royal Army Service Corps (Territorial Army) in Scotland performed the "Retreat" ceremony on Edinburgh Castle Esplanade on 27th May.

The bands were those of the 51st (H) Infantry Divisional Column, the 52nd (L) Infantry Divisional Column and the 123rd Transport Column. The pipers of these bands wore the Red McDuff tartan but, whereas the men of the 51st Highland Division were distinguished by their green doublets, those from the two Lowland units wore blue doublets. The drummers of the bands all wore R.A.S.C. No. 1 Dress. This was the first time these bands had performed together.

The Gurkha Army Service Corps, September 1959. The sixth of August, 1958, was an historic occasion for on that day there was born in the Far East within the Brigade of Gurkhas, a sister service — the Gurkha Army Service Corps.

Two Brigade Group Companies and two M.T. Companies will be formed and the initial cadres for one of each of these Companies commenced training at the R.A.S.C. School (Far East), Nee Soon, on 6th August, 1958.

Donald Peers, March 1960. The day an R.A.S.C. soldier sang at Buckingham Palace. A lot of water has babbled in that brook since Sgt. Donald Peers collected his leave pass and went along to the recording studio to wax the song which became his famous signature tune. It was nineteen years ago, in the middle of an air raid. The baron of ballads was an R.A.S.C. clerk working in a branch of the War Office.

Queen's Cup Won for First Time, July 1960. History was made by the R.A.S.C. at this year's Windsor Horse Show. For the first time ever, the Corps rode off with the Queen's Challenge Cup for Services' team jumping. It was a dramatic win for Major G. Boon, Major T. J. Brown and Sgt. Bob Graham, of Horse Transport Company at Buller Barracks, Aldershot.

Special Air Service, January 1961. Although a comparatively small unit, 22 Special Air Service Regiment at Hereford, has the honour of being blessed with no fewer than an officer

Well if it isnt the great Houdini

and fifteen other ranks of the R.A.S.C. The standard required is very exacting and all clerks with only two exceptions are parachute trained.

Kitbag, May 1961. By next year the familiar Army kitbag will be a thing of the past, and in its place will reign the suitcase. This innovation, perhaps distrusted by some of the "old soldiers," but welcomed enthusiastically by the majority, is one of many in the all-out recruiting drive, that is taking place.

ABOVE: The Corps coach, driven by Colonel James Burgess in Beaumont Barracks, 1968. The riding school was used in the film *Charge of the Light Brigade* for the church service and flogging. (L) BELOW: The *Gordon* and the Staff Band of the RCT on the occasion of the closing of the 64 year old Longmoor Military Railway, October 1969.

Castlemartin, 19 Company R.A.S.C. (Tank Transporter), November 1961. In spite of our normally placid outlook we were agreeably excited in August on being told that we were to be responsible for the U.K. movement of the West German tank unit which was to undergo training in Wales. Here was a task which was obviously an important one as far as Anglo-West German relations were concerned and one that would allow us, in our small way, to make a direct contribution to the NATO alliance. Equally obvious was the fact that the move would attract considerable publicity in every known form.

Corporal Missile, July 1962. High on the hill, overlooking the damp depressing German industrial centre of Wuppertal, lives a highly specialized R.A.S.C. unit, the Corps "Guided Weapons" Company.

Traffic often comes to a halt when the sixty-foot, loaded missile transporters of 111 Company, R.A.S.C. (G.W.) trundle out of Bangor Barracks for a tough, demanding driver-training run through the Ruhr or perhaps a few days in the field on exercise. But whatever the case the driver is the man solely responsible for a few thousand pounds worth of equipment.

Army Motor Cycling Championships, January 1963. 1 Training Battalion motor cyclists were in winning mood again in 1962, in spite of early season doubts as to whether the team would be strong enough owing to the departure of our National Service "aces" in Cpl. Vince, L./Cpl. Coppuch and Dvr. Griggs and of Sgt. Medland who left in March for civilian life.

There remained, however, Capt. Ovenden, Dvrs. Cullen, Hunter and Spackman, and Cpl Soames who was posted in during January, on whom to build for the coming season. The soundness of this foundation was well proved by our subsequent successes which culminated in the winning of the Army Championships for the second successive year, a feat achieved once before only, in the history of the competition.

Junior Tradesmen's Regiment Troon, March 1963. This Regiment, like its sister regiment in Rhyl, was formed in May last year to train boys as clerks, drivers/radio operators for eight different regiments and corps. The Regiment has not yet reached its full complement of trainees, but in view of the trades involved it is not surprising that, of the 350 boys at present under training, 97 belong to the Corps.

"Surely there must be some sport you are interested in?"

Institute of Advanced Motorists, August 1963. Sgt. R. W. G. Hanning of 6 Training Battalion recently qualified in the Commercial Vehicle Section of the Institute of Advanced Motorists test. He is the first member of the Armed Forces to do so.

The exacting two hours test included driving through towns and country, tight turns in very confined areas, reversing under every conceivable hazard and a commentary drive. The test was taken in a standard three-ton Bedford R.L. and strict observance of the Highway Code was required throughout.

ABOVE: Hovercraft of 200 Squadron comes in to land on one of Hong Kong's remote islands, 1969. (G) BELOW: An unusual view of Driver Douglas Munro in a line of 10 ton AEC 'Knockers', 27 Regiment, Bulford, October 1970. (G)

The Depot, February 1964. Contrary to popular belief, The Depot R.A.S.C. is still thriving, and it Officers have not lost the ability to put pen to paper provided the cause is just.

In November The Depot left Bordon and settled down in Aldershot occupying the "Tramlines". As a result of the move, The Depot reorganized, and took on many of the administrative tasks of 1 Training Battalion. The phrase "in November The Depot left Bordon" conjures up a picture of complete calm, amazing efficiency and thoughtful planning. However, the scenes in Bordon and Aldershot in mid-November were anything but calm, but in spite of teething troubles over who owned what, the outcome should prove satisfactory to all concerned.

Canoe Race, June 1965. On 17th April 1965, 63 Company became one of the few Army Units ever to win the Devizes to Westminster race. Dvrs Cook and Stimpson won in the magnificent time of 20 hours 27 minutes, beating the Royal Marine record holders into second place by 1 hour 11 minutes.

Rebadging, August 1965. Message to All Ranks from Field-Marshal H.R.H. The Duke of Gloucester, Earl of Ulster K.G., K.T., K.P., G.C.B., G.C.M.G., G.C.V.O. A.D.C.(D). Colonel-in-Chief Royal Corps of Transport

"On this historic day (15 July 1965), from which date it has been decreed Her Majesty The Queen that The Royal Army Service Corps shall be designated the Royal Corps of Transport, I send best wishes to all ranks of the Royal Corps of Transport wherever they may be serving.

In so doing, I wish to take this opportunity to say goodbye to those officers and men of The Royal Army Service Corps who have now transferred to the Royal Army Ordnance Corps and to welcome those of the Corps of Royal Engineers who have today joined the Royal Corps of Transport."

The Keys of Portsmouth, June 1966. Since 1961 the keys have been held by the Commanders Water Transport Group, R.A.S.C., and latterly by Commanders Maritime Group, R.C.T.

Maritime Group R.C.T., August 1966. Headquarters. — Perhaps the most important piece of news during the past two months has been that the Group is expected to form the first Army Hovercraft unit early in the New Year. Having lost our target towing launches with their speeds of 35 knots some years ago, it is good to hear that we will be back again in the realms of high speed where to cruise unconcerned at 60 knots could be normal practice.

The Group Commander and several officers

"And now the first thing I want you to do is . . ."
"I know, Sarge, I know—change the colour of my blanco."

attended the Hovershow at Browndown in June 1966 to obtain a private view of these craft. To accentuate this event, L.C.T. *Audemer* (Major A. Pheby) has taken a hovercraft to B.A.O.R. It sat comfortably on two beams bridging the tank deck, and looked like a contented duck. A full load of vehicles was shipped at the same time.

ABOVE: 'Ole Bill' on its way to the Imperial War Museum, April 1970, driven by 80-year-old George Gwynn, who drove similar LGOC omnibuses on the Western Front in the Great War. (M) RIGHT: 14 Air Despatch Regiment changing guard at Buckingham Palace, February 1973. Major Pat Reid, late RASC, of Colditz fame, looks on. BELOW: Ken Howard paints 3 Tank Transporter Squadron in Moscow Camp, Belfast, 1975. Sgt Paterson and Cpl Fullerton stand in as models. RIGHT: Captain Peter Marshall (150 (Northumbrian) Transport Regiment (V)), Champion Shot at Bisley TA Skill-at-Arms Meeting, 1986. (N).

130 Flight, October 1966. The Flight continues to operate in three locations — Singapore, Brunei and Tawau. In spite of the gradual easing of confrontation, most of the flying is still carried out in the two Borneo detachments where in the last two months over 500 hours were flown in support of Central and West Brigades.

The flying has remained as varied as ever; casualty evacuation (including one by night), air O.P., and supply dropping sorties have all been carried out during the last two months along with the continuing heavy commitment to communication flying.

Malaya, December 1966. The end of "confrontasi" and of the "roulement" which went with it has naturally been particularly welcomed in this Command. Who, we wonder, first introduced that expressive but unlikely word "roulement"? The British Army always seems to coin some new phrase or piece of jargon for each of its campaigns and this particular one, with its overtones of turbulence and instability, will we hope not have to be perpetuated in some other theatre.

Housewives, February 1967. It has been noticed on several recent Boards of Survey that empty housewives are being put up for disposal by unit Quartermasters. This procedure is incorrect. Housewives when they become empty will be refilled by demanding refills as necessary from R.A.O.C. Only housewives which are unserviceable will be submitted on Boards for Survey in future. Extracted from Garrison Order 359/59 (overseas station).

The Army Ensign. In October 1966, Her Majesty The Queen graciously gave permission for ships of the Army flying the Army ensign, commanded by officers and manned by Army personnel in uniform to be designated "Her Majesty's Army Vessels" and to fly the Union Flag at the fore when the ship is moored or under way and wearing masthead flags.

At that time no Army ensign existed. The ensign of the Royal Corps of Transport fleet only was worn. The design of the Army ensign was recently approved by the Defence Council and consists of the Blue Ensign containing the Army badge of Crossed Swords surmounted by the Crown and Lion. This badge was presented to the Army by King George VI in 1938.

is for the FAMILY CAR

The modern small car works hard for its living. It's the family man's best friend, his beast of burden, the apple of his eye. And now, with its modern high-compression engine, it can give the sort of sports-car performance that makes driving a real joy.

But high-compression engines are liable to knock, and as compression ratios go up and up, so does the need for higher-octane fuel which will prevent this knocking. In fact, modern engine development would not be possible without high-octane petrols. And Super Shell, the most advanced of them all, has added I.C.A., something special to ensure that your car makes the best possible use of high octane. This is why Super Shell is now an essential part of happy family motoring

Go like Super SHELL

(SHELL) you can be S for SURE of it

Buller Barracks Unveiling Ceremony, September 1967. On Wednesday, 26th July, we were honoured by a visit from our Colonel-in-Chief who had kindly consented to unveil a memorial plaque on the site of one of the new buildings in Buller Barracks. At noon H.R.H. The Duke of Gloucester accompanied by the Representative Colonel Commandant, Major-General P. G. Turpin, arrived at the site where a distinguished gathering of spectators was assembled.

After the unveiling a fanfare, specially composed by the Director of Music, was

Ramp Powered Lighter of 10 Port Squadron loading a Bedford RL of 58
Squadron, alongside HMS *Bulwark*, Cyprus, 1973. (O)

sounded by the trumpeters of the Staff Band and the Duke of Gloucester then made a short speech.

20 Squadron, November 1967. During September Regents Park Barracks was turned into a little Hollywood as cameras, horses, actors, actresses and technicians together with all the vehicles necessary for film making took over half the barracks to take a few scenes for the film *"The Charge of the Light Brigade"*. At last everything from the film world has gone, leaving us to concentrate on our transport details.

The Name is "Morley", May 1968. Dvr. John Morley, who enlisted in September last year as a regular soldier, has recently completed his recruit training at 12 Training Regt., and follows in the footsteps of his great grandfather, Pte. Samuel Morley of 2nd Battalion Military Train who was awarded the Victoria Cross over one hundred years ago in 1858.

90 Squadron, September 1968. One of the more interesting Squadron tasks recently has been the re-supply of aviation fuel to Nizwa which is situated high up in the Jebel El Akhdar in Muscat and Oman. The fuel has been required for helicopters operating in support of infantry patrols in the area.

Northern Ireland, November 1969. 26 Squadron. — Since our last literary efforts, the tempo of life has changed dramatically. When the situation in Northern Ireland became critical on 15th August, 1969, approximately 4,000 reinforcements were brought in. As the only R.C.T. unit in Northern Ireland it fell to us to transport them from the airport and docks to their bases — in one case straight into the streets of Belfast.

Depot Regiment, January 1970. The period since our last notes has been taken up primarily with preparation for the forthcoming move into the new Buller Barracks. The move itself is now under way

and parts of the Regiment are currently "moving house" back to the "ancestral" home; the move to be completed by 23rd November.

The change in location also signals the start of a new role for the Regiment. We are now going to assume responsibility for providing centralised administrative services throughout the R.C.T. Training Centre in Aldershot. The concept is that we administer whilst 12 Regiment trains. The Regiment will still retain its Depot function which will continue to be carried out by P Squadron.

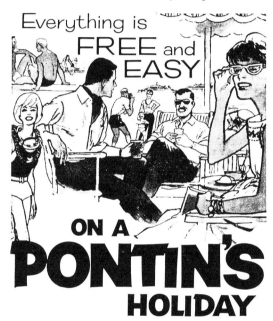

'H' Squadron, March 1970. Many readers will be very sad to learn of the Army decision to disband H Squadron R.C.T. at the end of March, 1970. This will mean that, apart from some pack transport in Hong Kong the Corps' age old association with animal transport in all its forms will come to an end.

Freedom of Aldershot, May 1970. On Wednesday, 22nd April, 1970, the Freedom of the Borough of Aldershot was presented to

ABOVE: 'Gawd! What we animals have to suffer at the hands of men!'
LCpl Leung Kam Chong and Sgt Healy of 414 Pack Troop in Hong Kong
do their best to secure the load. (G) BELOW: Britain's answer to the
Russian steamroller: 8 Regiment 'dressed to kill' during the annual
inspection, Munster 1973.

the Royal Corps of Transport by the Mayor, Alderman and Burgesses of the Borough of Aldershot. The proceedings commenced with a parade, commanded by Lieut.-Colonel R. J. Royle with Lieut.-Colonel J. Radcliffe as Chief Marshal, in the Recreation Ground, Aldershot.

There were six squadrons of marching troops (three squadrons provided by 12 Training Regiment and one each from No. 2 Transport Group, 7 Squadron and 17 Squadron) with the Staff Band and the Corps of Drums from 12 Training Regiment. The troops keeping the Ground were provided by H Squadron and this was its last public appearance before disbandment was completed. In addition to the troops on parade, a cavalcade of vehicles, representing a cross section of the activities of the R.C.T. and provided by 3 Divisional Regiment and 2 Transport Group, joined the parade as it marched through the centre of Aldershot.

Bank of England Guard, May 1971. On Saturday 9 January, 63 Parachute Squadron became the first Corps unit to provide the picquet to guard the Bank of England. The Squadron, as part of 2nd Battalion The Parachute Regiment Group, was given this honour during the battalion term of public duties in January and February of this year.

Winter Olympics, March 1972. Cpl. Keith Oliver of H.Q. 27 Regiment has been selected to race for Great Britain in the forthcoming Winter Olympics at Sapporo in Japan.

He is the reigning British biathlon champion and has been a member of the British team for the past three years.

Malta, July 1972. 32 Transport and Movements Squadron. — These will be our last notes as the unit disbanded on 28 March 1972 due to the Malta withdrawal and subsequent rationalisation. However, notes will still be sent from Malta by the Army element of the JSPU. Not unnaturally the last months of the Squadron were taken up with withdrawal of British Troops from the island.

22 Squadron. It is not often nowadays that a new squadron is formed but here we are in Erskine Barracks, Wilton, a staff car squadron in support of HQ UKLF, which includes five Generals, 20 Brigadiers and a host of lesser mortals. Members of the Corps will appreciate the fun and games keeping such people happy.

The London Public Duties Commitment. At 11.30 am on Sunday 25 February 1973 a detachment of 14 Air Despatch Regiment RCT, accompanied by the Staff Band and the

Talk about Alvis...

and you are talking about the Stalwart, specifically developed into a High Mobility Load Carrier for the British Army. Its purpose is to replenish all combat arms - including tanks - in every part of the world, often over extreme terrain conditions. Its performance compares with most tracked vehicles. Amphibious, it is completely capable of operating in open sea as well as inland water.

...talk about outstanding cross-country vehicles

ALVIS OF COVENTRY ENGLAND STALWART

Corps of Drums created a precedent in our history. Watched by many serving and retired members of the Corps, and by many visitors to London, the RCT contingent marched into the forecourt of Buckingham Palace to take over the duties of the Queen's Guard.

Ski-ing Triumphs, May 1973. The hopes of past and present Corps skiers were realised this season when 2 Divisional Regiment RCT won the coveted Princess Marina, Duchess of Kent Cup for the first time in ski-ing history, warding off the fierce traditional challenge of the Gunners and Sappers.

ABOVE: HRH Princess Alice, Duchess of Gloucester, visits 27 Regiment in Bulford, accompanied by Colonel Rupert Wallis (CO) and Major-General John Carpenter (Representative Colonel Commandant), April 1976. BELOW: Drum Major Jimmy Gray leads the Pipes and Drums of 153 (Highland) Regiment (V) in Munster, 1979.

14 Air Despatch Regiment, Khana Cascade, July 1973. With regimental participation in London Public Duties fading fast into history attention was focussed on Nepal, where famine conditions of astronomic proportions prevail as a result of successive failures of the rice crop. To alleviate some of the suffering, the assistance of the British Government was sought and in response to this call Hercules of 46 Group RAF accompanied by despatchers of 14 AD Regt established bases in Nepal, from which they undertook the delivery of 2000 tons of rice in six weeks.

Northern Ireland, March 1974. You will find soldiers of the RCT wherever you go in Northern Ireland. Not only are they doing their normal job of moving and supplying the Army on the roads, in the docks and at the airfields, but you will also find them driving armoured vehicles in direct support of battalions and, on occasions, patrolling as infantrymen. Our major assistance in this field has been to drive the Armoured Personnel Carriers (APCs). These are the six wheeled Saracen and the Humber one ton armoured, or "Pig" as the latter is universally called because of both looks and handling characteristics.

Hovercraft, May 1974. Sadly this will be the last mention of 200 Hovercraft Trials Squadron RCT. The Army Board has decided to discontinue Army hovercraft trials, and the unit ceased to operate with effect from 31 March. Since its formation in 1966, the Squadron has had a very varied existence, visiting such countries as Australia, Singapore, Borneo, Japan, Turkey, Norway, Denmark, Germany, France and Belgium as well as the Channel Islands and Scotland, including the Hebrides.

DUKWs, July 1974. April 19, 1974: a memorable day in the history of our Corps, for it was the final parade of the DUKW. The last remaining section of this veteran of Messina, South East Asia and Normandy was finally disbanded at a parade at 17 Port Regiment, Marchwood. For this nostalgic occasion we were extremely honoured to have Admiral of the Fleet, Earl Mountbatten of Burma, KG, take the salute; and how appropriate, for it was he, as Chief of Combined Operations in 1942, who made the decision to obtain the DUKW for our forces.

we're on ops now

WITH THE WORLD'S FIRST FULLY-OPERATIONAL HOVERCRAFT SQUADRON

BHC hovercraft have now joined the forces - as regulars enlisted for active service, at home and abroad, with the Royal Corps of Transport Hovercraft Squadron. This vital decision by the British Government to purchase BHC SR.N6's for the world's first fully-operational hovercraft squadron, marks the full establishment of hovercraft as front-line vehicles with a vital role in military operations and will undoubtedly influence defence planning throughout the world.

BHC hovercraft lead the world. Incorporating systems and components proven in over 20,000 hours of operation all over the world, the 10 ton SR.N6 carries 30 fully equipped troops or over 3 tons of freight, and is able to mount the latest weapons systems. It cruises at 56 knots and is unrestricted by reefs, sandbanks, underwater defences, ice, tide state or shallows, giving military forces a freedom and speed of movement by day or night far in advance of anything feasible for conventional craft.

BHC hovercraft are the only hovercraft that have been used on military operations - both by British Defence Forces and by the U.S. Navy. They have proved themselves in extremes of climatic conditions, from tropical jungles and deserts to the frozen arctic - from Sweden to Sarawak, from Thailand to the far north of Canada. BHC strength is further emphasised by the recent Government decision to order both the fast attack and the logistic amphibious versions of the larger 40 ton BH.7. The 10 ton SR.N6 is in full production with the 40 ton BH.7 to follow shortly.

BRITISH HOVERCRAFT - WORLD LEADERS IN THE HOVER TRANSPORT REVOLUTION

british hovercraft corporation limited
YEOVIL ENGLAND

Electric Car Trials, 23 Transport and Movements Regiment, January 1975. The past two months have seen the continuation of the experiments with the TO in C (A)'s electric trials car (which we have now passed to 24 Tpt and Mov Regt for further evaluation), the acquiring of new ambulance rolling stock, and involvement in the Cyprus emergency.

Customer reaction to the electric car was on the whole favourable, and after the first odd, plaintive cries of 'help!' from operators who had unexpectedly run out of power, the trial quickly settled into a routine and the car became a familiar sight in the purlieus of Moenchengladbach and Rheindahlen.

ABOVE: First Annual Dinner of the Coventry Branch of the RASC/RCT Association, February 1984: Lt-Col and Mrs Bert Hallows, Mr Roberts (Chairman), Major-General and Mrs John Carpenter and Mrs Roberts. (P) BELOW: Major Peterson and WO2 Hodgson, 10 Port Squadron, at the Akrotiri Mole, Cyprus, 1986. The launch *Michael Murphy VC* is leaving harbour; Ramped Craft Logistic vessels *Arromanches* and *Antwerp* remain.

The Worshipful Company of Carmen of London, September 1975. On 23 July 1975 at a meeting of the Court of Assistants of the Worshipful Company of Carmen of London, held at Grocers Hall, Princess Street, London EC2, Articles of Association were exchanged between the Worshipful Company of Carmen and senior representatives of the Royal Corps of Transport.

Hong Kong (UPI), January 1976. There were no tears, for that wouldn't be in keeping with the best traditions of the British Army. Their commander patted and scratched each of them individually, a final tribute for a job well done. The inspection and other formalities over, Lt Gen Sir Edwin Bramall, Commander of the British Forces in Hong Kong., worked up a smile, said 'thank you', and quickly marched off. There were no speeches.

The solemn occasion was the official disbandment of 414 Pack Transport Troop of the Royal Corps of Transport, the last mule unit of the British Forces. It was in keeping with the British policy of phasing out its defence presence east of Suez. It ended a glorious tradition dating back to 1914.

Modern Pentathlon, October 1976. The gold medal won by the British modern pentathlon team in the recent Olymic Games was a magnificent effort of which Britain can be proud. One person who must be more than delighted is Maj Gen E H G Lonsdale, CB, MBE, who is chairman of the Modern Pentathlon Association of Great Britain. During his service career, Gen Lonsdale was particularly keen on the modern pentathlon as a sport which demands a high degree of physical fitness and mental ability. He did much to raise the standards of this sport in both the RASC/RCT and at Army levels.

Cyprus UN Tour, 8 Squadron. It is hard to realise that the squadron is approaching the half-way mark of the tour as part of the United Nations Force in Cyprus. It has been a most enjoyable tour and, for our younger soldiers, just what the recruiting posters advertised!

The first difficulty the squadron experienced was getting used to the local terminology and jargon. Camp UNFICYP, BBC CAMP, Sector One, Section Six, AUSCON, CANCON, Checkpoint Foxtrot, Checkpoint Patricia, the list is endless.

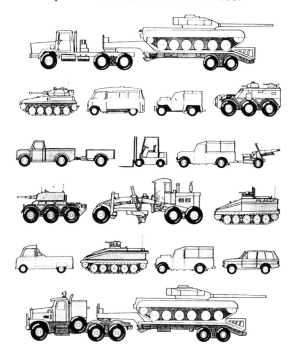

BRITISH LEYLAND MILITARY VEHICLES

Back-bone of the modern army

An army today must be totally mobile. As well as armoured vehicles, it needs transporters to carry them, heavy lorries and transport of every shape and size for the movement of troops and equipment, fork lift trucks to relieve man power, road making equipment to smooth out difficult terrain.
British Leyland makes them all. Plus the power systems to keep them going.

 **Military Products**

Lord Mayor's Show, 151 (Greater London) Regiment, March 1977. One of the highlights of London's calendar is the Lord Mayor's Show. For the second successive year, the regiment had the distinction of taking part in the procession. This year's theme was 'The City and the Sea' and our entry was a viking longship drawn by a tank transporter. It demonstrated to the watching and viewing television public the Corps' links with London and two of its roles, namely, driving and

LEFT: Even drivers in the most excellent of regiments occasionally have problems with soft shoulders. A Thorneycroft Antar of 7 Tank Transporter Regiment at Hasperde in 1983. RIGHT: Movers in the Falkland Islands, 1984: Sgt Colin Pressley's unit insisted that the penguin sign was not on the door of the Joint Services Movements Staff. BELOW: A Mexeflote of 73 (Falkland Islands) Squadron helps to put down moorings for temporary floating accommodation at Canache, July 1983.

sailing. The longship was provided by 20 Maritime Regiment at Gosport and made a splendid and eyecatching float.

Association Rally, December 1977. Our Golden Jubilee Rally was attended by some 2800 on 1 October. Displays were given by the Depot and Training Regiment, the Junior Leaders Regiment, 153 (Highland) and 154 (Lowland) Regiment TAVR, the Bedfordshire Army Cadet Force (RCT-affiliated cadets) and the whole impressive event was supported by the Staff Band of the Royal Corps of Transport. This military pageant was a clear indication to the old soldiers of how the modern Army so ably and efficiently carries out its task. The ENSA-type show was given by Miss Anne Shelton, Mr Cardew Robinson and Mr Billy "Uke" Scott, and we are grateful to them for making their part a success.

Army Footballer of the Year, September 1978. Cpl David Blanche, serving with the Depot and Training Regiment at Buller Barracks, is the 1978 Army Footballer of the Year. Cpl Blanche, an assistant physical training instructor, was presented with the trophy by Gen Sir James Wilson, KBE, MC, president of the Army Football Association, at the annual dinner and dance at the end of last season.

Waterloo Action Commemorated, September 1979. One hundred and sixty-four years after the Battle of Waterloo, Wellington and Napoleon would have found that the seasonal weather had changed very little and on 14 June 1979 on a cold and wet day, a memorial plaque was dedicated at Hougoumont Farm to commemorate the presence of the Royal Waggon Train at that part of the battle. This presence was significantly marked by Private Brewster, who, with a tumbril of ammunition and with great gallantry, drove straight down to the farm under heavy fire, to deliver the ammunition to the 3rd Guards and thus help save the day.

British Army Training Unit, Suffield. Probably, the most interesting of the

movement control tasks is the loading and discharge of our tanks, ammunition, vehicles and other heavy equipments to and from LSLs and RFAs operating through the west coast ports of Vancouver and Prince Rupert. These equipments are moved to and from the base by rail through the spectacular Rocky Mountains.

The detachment is also responsible for running and controlling the live firing exercises for the RCT elements of the battle group echelons. This is very realistic training which concentrates on defended positions.

& National Westminster Bank

Motor Cycling, March 1980. The Corps is lucky to have had a number of excellent motor-cyclists in the past, and most readers who are interested in two-wheeled sport will know of the excellent riding ability of Sgt G Webb (now TA) who has been Army Champion seven times, and Cpl A Barraclough, transferred from REME to RCT, who is a strong, dedicated and very professional rider. Barraclough has had many successes, including a gold award in the Welsh two-day Enduro in June.

ABOVE: Junior Leaders Passing Out Parade, August 1983: Major-General Derek Braggins, Director-General Transport and Movements, talks to Junior LCpl Noble, Mascot LCpl Taku's handler, while Lt-Col Charles Colvin gives the animal a wide berth. (Q) BELOW: 27 Regiment provides the Guard of Honour for HM The Queen on 18 July 1988 at the Royal Tournament, Earls Court.

I would like to turn the spotlight on Dvr Wayne Buckley, known to his friends as Bill, who is serving in 2 Armoured Division Transport Regiment. Buckley is a cheerful, hard-riding, 23-year-old who first rode a motor-cycle in Junior Leaders Regiment RCT and has ridden in competitions since November 1975.

Northern Ireland, March 1981. The Country APC Squadron. — The characteristic whine of the Rolls Royce Saracen engine will now no longer be heard within the confines of HMP Maze, SF Base. In November 1980, 11 Squadron, the last country APC squadron to be based in the Maze, redeployed from Long Kesh to Belfast.

During the recent four and a half month roulement tour, the squadron deployed its APCs and drivers throughout the Province. In November the squadron headquarters moved from Long Kesh to Moscow Camp in Belfast, to join the regimental headquarters of the APC roulement regiment and the squadron headquarters city APC squadron.

Quartermaster-General, March 1982. In 1888, Gen Sir Redvers Buller, then Quartermaster-General at the War Office, insisted that the supply and transport units should be staffed by officers of high calibre, wearing the same uniform and badges as their men. The effect resulted in the formation, in 1889, of a fully combatant Army Service Corps, with its horse transport depot at Woolwich and its supply and regimental depots at Aldershot.

In his memorandum on the formation of the Army Service Corps in 1888 Gen Sir Redvers Buller, the QMG, wrote as follows: . . .

"I can see no reason why Army Service Corps officers should not look forward to the day when it shall be open to them to sit in the chair I now occupy."

Lt-Gen Sir Paul Travers, KCB, assumed the appointment of Quartermaster-General on 8 March 1982. The sentiments expressed by Gen Buller in 1888 have, therefore, been fulfilled.

Junior Leaders Regiment, March 1983. The December end-of-term parade saw the promotion of the longest-serving junior leader in the regiment. J/DVR Taku, the regimental pet Shetland pony, rose to the rank of J/LCPL. It was considered that after three troublesome years with the regiment, Taku had achieved a high standard, both in his work and behaviour. In spite of his lack of aptitude as far as driving goes, he was recommended for this well-deserved promotion.

Viva Award, September 1983. The back-up provided by the Royal Corps of Transport for the Task Force during the Falklands operations has been honoured by the

Worshipful Company of Carmen with their Viva award for 'outstanding service'. The award together with a gold medal and citation, was presented to Maj-Gen D H Braggins, DGTM, by the Master of the Carmen's Company, Mr C A Hart, in London on 14 July. The citation accompanying the award praised the Corps' improvisation and inventiveness in overcoming problems of 'daunting complexity' in transport by land, sea and air.

ABOVE: Drivers Munro and Donald of 63 Squadron cleaning their rifles on exercise, 1989. RIGHT: Sgt Sidhiman Rai GTR holds the McDonald Trophy as the piper who contributed most to piping in the Brigade of Gurkhas, 1987. Cpl Kamalbahadur Gurung, the senior drummer, looks on. BELOW: Sgt Kevin Perkins, 1988 Army Footballer of the Year, holds aloft the Army Challenge Cup won by 10 Corps Transport Regiment in 1989. (K) RIGHT: Part-time women soldiers of 151 (Greater London) Transport Regiment (V) attack a 10 ft wall during the 1991 London District Courage Trophy competition. (R)

The Corps made a major contribution to the operation by moving men and materiel over an 8,000-mile line of communication. The citation also points out the contribution made to the rehabilitation of the islanders after the conflict. It concludes 'The Corps' outstanding planning skills, adaptability and professionalism played a significant part in the success of the campaign and resulted in many transportation developments of potential military and civil use.

Falkland Islands, June 1984. 73(FI) Port Squadron. It can never be said that life in the Falklands is uneventful and with the constant struggle for normalization, life is made all the more interesting. The Falklands intermediate port and storage facilities (FIPASS) are here and we have just moved into our new locations, bidding a sad farewell to the Falkland Islands Company offices we have occupied since the end of the conflict. Our REME Workshop and Plant Section have also moved to a new Romney at the Canache at the eastern end of the harbour. B Slip is very much in operation but this will eventually be phased out as more supplies and ships come direct to FIPASS. The introduction of FIPASS has seen squadron headquarters moving into plush new office accommodation and Port Troop getting a Portakabin beside the FIPASS RO-RO.

Belfast, September 1984. After twelve years the sutler contract in Moscow Camp has been ended. Thousands of our Corps soldiers have passed through Moscow Camp, home of numerous Op Banner roulement squadrons during the years, and since 1975 the sutler contract has been held by Mr 'King' Ghulan Hussain, a Pathan born in 1935 and now a British subject, who has had a colourful life following the flag. For much of this time he has served RASC and RCT units in Cyprus and Northern Ireland.

His earliest memories are of working outside Bombay in 1944 where, as char wallah with his father, he served soldiers of 1st Wing. This formation is unknown to the author, but

King recollects that they were billeted in Durnah Camp, or Camp 44. After Indian Independence they remained with the Indian Army but, in June 1956, came to Famagusta in Cyprus and among their principal customers were 6 Company. In 1958 they moved to Episkopi and looked after the needs of 58 Company until 1960 when 'King', by this time a British subject, made a new life in England.

MCTG, September 1985. The fortieth anniversary of the formation of Mobile Civilian Transport Units (MCTG) was celebrated at a special parade held at Wrexham Barracks, Mulheim, on 6 July. At the parade, five veterans were each presented with special certificates commemorating their forty years of service with the RASC and RCT by the Director-General of Transport and Movements, Maj-Gen D H Braggins, on behalf of the Commnander-in-Chief BAOR. He also presented nineteen long-serving members of MCTG, who joined British service

ABOVE: Presentation of the Viva Shield to the Corps for achievement and innovation in the Falklands by Master of the Carmen's Company of London, Past Sheriff Tony Hart, to the DGTM Maj-Gen Derek Braggins, 1983. BELOW: Challenger tanks deploy from tank transporters of 7 Tank Transporter Regiment, in the Gulf, 1991.

151

in 1945 and will also complete forty years service this year, with special certificates marking their participation in the parade.

Two War Veterans Meet at Antwerp, September 1986. The *Sir Tristram,* survivor of the attack on Bluff Cove during the Falklands conflict, came to the aid of another war veteran on its way home, a French cannon that had been captured by the British over 170 years earlier at the Battle of Waterloo. Thanks to the Royal Corps of Transport the ancient cannon, called La Suffisance, arrived at the docks in Antwerp recently, nearing the end of a journey which began days before at the Tower of London.

Falklands Port Opened. The Services of the Falkland Islands are moving from Stanley to Mount Pleasant and East Cove complex as the building of that establishment progresses. 73 (FI) Port Squadron is very much involved.

To support the giant Mount Pleasant complex (MPC) a new port has been built at East Cove some six miles south of the new airport. The port is run by 73 Squadron and manned by a detachment commanded by Capt Cecilia Flint. The port was handed over by the contractors and officially opened by the DGTM, Maj-Gen D B H Colley, CBE, on Wednesday 12 November 1986.

Silver Despatch Rider, June 1986. On 21 February a new piece of silver was acquired by the Corps with the arrival of 4 Armoured Division Transport Regiment of a silver Canam and despatch rider. It was commissioned by the regiment from silversmith Keith Tasker in late 1984. Forty-nine past and present officers contributed to the cost of the item and the Corps Association very generously made a donation.

The despatch rider is incredibly detailed and flawless in its accuracy. It is a fitting memento of a soon-to-disappear machine, and recognizes the resurgence of motorcycles in the operations of the Corps.

REME Drivers Transfer to the Corps, June 1988. 1 April 1988 was a special day in that it was the date of transfer of responsibility from REME to RCT for the provision of B vehicle drivers in REME workshops. Two hundred and twenty three REME all ranks rebadged and already two sergeants have been selected for promotion to staff sergeant; we are sure these are the first of many more promotions to come.

Football, May 1989. Wednesday 19 April 1989 was a great day in the sporting history of our Corps. 10 Corps Transport Regiment from Bielefeld won the Army Challenge Cup, beating the School of Signals 5-0 in the final, held, as ever, in the Military Stadium, Aldershot.

The Gulf, March 1991. 1 Armoured Division Transport Regiment has now fully deployed into the desert sands of Saudi Arabia. After an initial three weeks period in the infamous port sheds, RHQ, 2 Squadron, 33 Squadron and Echelon set off to deploy to their different locations out in the dry and dusty wastelands. Our task is to provide the logistic support to 7 Armoured Brigade and shortly also to 4 Armoured Brigade as they form up to become 1 (UK) Armoured Division.

10 Corps Transport Regiment was the focal point for the deployment of third line RCT support on Op Granby. Becoming 10 Regiment RCT Group Middle East we have taken under command 12 Squadron and 16 Squadron (−) and, for administration, 50 MC Squadron, which has in fact now returned to the UK, having been replaced by 59 MC Squadron, and last but not least 52 Port Squadron. We have been extremely busy in the Gulf in support of the Force Maintenance Area and of course 7 Armoured Brigade. The CO, Lt-Col P Chaganis, and the RSM, WO1 MacLachlan, were among the very first British elements to arrive in theatre and, besides establishing the regiment, were almost solely responsible for meeting and sorting out the entire force, heading up the reception party.

ABOVE: Standards of the RASC/RCT Association are lowered in salute at the Corps Memorial, Buller Barracks, during Corps Weekend, 1987. Major-General Pat Claxton leads the Old Comrades. (G) BELOW: Backwards into the future: Driver Stephen in 'the good ship RCT', Priddy's Hard, Gosport, 1986. (G)

INDEX TO PHOTOGRAPHS

PHOTOGRAPH ACKNOWLEDGEMENTS

The author is grateful to the following for their kind permission to use their photographs: Peter Hicks, Kevin Lee, Richard Till, Richard Watt, *Soldier Magazine*, *The Times*, *Aldershot Gazette*, the *Bath Evening Chronicle* and the *Coventry Citizen*. Other photographers or sources are listed below, 'several of them defunct or otherwise untraceable. He apologises to anyone whose copyright he has inadvertently infringed. Sources are annotated with key letters. Where a photograph is published with no key letter the source is regrettably not known. H. W. Leach, Aldershot (A), Gale and Polden, Aldershot (B), M. Bennett, Ladysmith (C), J. Thomson, North Camp (D), Henry Linn, Woolwich (E), W. M. May, Aldershot (F), Crown Copyright (G), Star Photos, Perth (H), Reader and Ward, Aldershot (I), P. McEntire, London (J), *Soldier Magazine*, Aldershot (K), Sport and General London, (L), *The Times* (M), Mr Peter Hicks, Woking (N), Mr Richard Till, Witchford (O), *Coventry Citizen* (P), *Bath Evening Chronicle* (Q), Mr Richard Watt, London, (R), Mr Kevin Lee, Liphook, (S), *Motor Cycling* (T).

SUBSCRIBERS

I HRH Princess Alice, Duchess of Gloucester GCB, CI, GCVO, GBE
II Institution of the Royal Corps of Transport
III Royal Australian Corps of Transport
IV Royal New Zealand Corps of Transport
V Army Service Corps of India
VI Army Service Corps of Pakistan
VII The Sri Lanka Army Service Corps
VIII The Malaysian Service Corps
IX The Worshipful Company of Carmen

1 Lt Col M.H.G. Young
2 Clive Birch FSA, FRSA
3 Lt Col J.G. Hambleton MBE
4 Maj Gen J.D. MacDonald CB, CBE
5 Maj Gen I.S. Baxter CBE
6 Maj Gen D.H. Braggins CB
7 Maj Gen D.B.H. Colley CB, CBE
8 Maj Gen C.E.G. Carrington CB, CBE
9 Sir Peter Levene KBE
10 Maj Gen D.L. Burden CBE
11 Lt Col C. Harvey
12 Maj L.A. Bower
13 Col N.E.L. Gilbert
14 Lt Col H. Lincoln Jones MBE
    BEng
15 Dvr R.J. Ford
16 S. Atkins
17 Maj W.K. Jewell
18 T.R. Whitley OStJ, OPR, OSJB, RMN
19 Col P.F. Hollins
20 J. Atlee
21 F.H.J. Brown
22 D. Boot
23 Lt Col D.J. Turner
24 Lt Col M.A. Willson-Lloyd
25 Sgt J.T. Campos
26 Lt Col I.H.W. Bennett
27 A.E. Street
28 WOI (RSM) P.N. Jerrard BEM MSM
29 Maj M.J. Boden LLB(Hons)
30 C.A. Pushong BA, FRGS
31 Maj T. Embury MBE
32 Maj R.A.D. Sinclair
33 Col H. Bentley-Marchant
34 Lt Cdr J.J. Town-Clear RNR
    SBOSJ
35 R. Mackinlay
36 Lt Col G.T. Pearce MBE
37 W.J. Reilly
38 Col B.G. Jones
39 Col R.F. Discombe OBE
40 SSgt J.R. Purves
41 Lt Col M.R.U. McCartney
42 D.J. Miller
43 Capt F. West
44 Maj R.H. Woodward TD
45 Lt Col D. Neighbour
46 Maj H.B. Stevens
47 WO2 M.P. Daddow
48 Dvr G.Y. Kenny
49 T.J. Jackson
50 W. Young
51 John Walker
52
53   Maj M.W. Everton MBE

54 WO2 J. Fraser
55 Dvr B. Wickes
56 Col J.S. Riggall MBE
57 Maj G.W. Murley
58 Maj J. Garwood
59 Capt M.A.D. Sears
60 K.H. Eastmond
61 W.A. Morris
62 Capt C.C. Powell
63 Maj G.H. Atkinson
64 Maj H.J. Reoch
65 Lt Col R. Millington
66 Maj J.S.R. Shave MC
67 Maj R.H. Stiles Allen
68 Maj E.P. Saunders RCT
69 Lt Col C.R.H. Wells
70 Maj R.A. Hill BEM
71 Capt K.B. Carey
72 Officers' Mess 153(H)
    Arty Sp Regt RCT (V)
73 Maj A.F. Neve
74 L.J. Aspland OBE
75 John Abbott
76 Lt Col A.G. Price
77 Coventry Branch RASC/RCT Assoc
78 Lt Col A.W. Hallows OBE
79 S.J. Stevens RASC
80 Maj (QM) W.K. Adrian RCT
81 Charles C. Stadden
82 Maj R.H. Dobson TD RCT(V)
83 155 (Wessex) Regiment 1965-1993
84 Maj R.M. Taylor
85 Sgt S.E. Dawe
86 Lt Col E.G. Waite-Roberts TD
87 Capt N.A. Smith (Retd)
88 Lt Col (QM) R.K. Cooley
89 Pte John R. Petherick
90 WO1 G. W. Barnes
91 Capt D. M. Russett
92 SSgt A. O'Brien
93 Brig W.R. Barker CBE
94 Col D.M. Gluckstein TD, DL
95 Col E.E. Bonner TD
96 Lt Col T.A. Danton-Rees
97 Maj Gen V.H.J. Carpenter CB, MBE
98 Maj Roy M. Rodgers TD
99 Lt Col R.E.T. Bulloch TD
100 WO1 (GSM) A.F. Flinn
102 Capt J.B. Mee
103 Maj G.A. Fitness
104 Hon Maj F.R.B. King
105 Maj D.J. Glossop Diptpm MCIT,
    MILDM, MITD
106 Col J.C. Lucas OBE
107 Maj Gen P.F. Claxton CB, OBE

108 Maj A.R. Grimshaw
109 Col G.T. Spate OBE, TD, DL
110 "Chippie" Wood
111 Maj D.J. Owen
112 Capt A.D. Jennings RCT
113 C.S. Stockdale
114 Capt M.J. Gartside
115 WO2 (SSM) A.J. Hanlon
116 WO1 K.J. Tweddle RCT
117 Lt Col E.A. Kynaston
118 Maj Gen A.F.J. Elmslie CB, CBE,
    FIMechE, FCIT
119 Capt J. Capeling
120 Capt A.R. Tysoe
121 Lt Col M.H.G. Young
122 A.J.G. Young BEM
123 Maj Gen E.H.G. Lonsdale CB, MBE
124 Maj Gen W. Bate CB, OBE, DL, FCIT
125 Maj (Retd) J.A. Collar
126 Bryan Wilkinson BEM
127 Maj M.B. Grey
128 Capt J.R.C. Craig
129 Brig A.F.R. Evans MBE
130 Maj I.W. Abbott
131 Capt John Venmore
132 WO1 J.R. Armstrong
133 Gordon F. Rintoul
134 Stan Farnell Ex-SSgt
135 Maj N. G. Campbell
136 Maj A.S. Bray
137 Maj Ray Pinnock
138 WO1 G. Binnington
139 Maj (Retd) G.T. Cook
140 Maj (QM) H.M. Whitehead
141 Maj G.M.K. Fraser MBIM
142 Brig E.W.T. Darlow OBE, MA, FCIT
    FBIM
143 SSgt E.T. Taylor
144 S.J. Walke
145 Mrs S.J. Walke
146 Maj Ted Lipscombe
147 WO1 B. Greenwood MBE
148 Capt T.G.W. Woodman
149 Col H.S. Butterworth MBE, MC, TD
150 Maj D.M. Bond MBE, JP, MCIT
151 Maj E.T. Chapple
152 Commander Transport, Detmold
    Garrison
153 Maj R.A. Dixon-Warren
154 Officers' Luncheon Club, 16 Tk Tptr
    Sqn RCT
155 Col H.V.C. Stephens
156 Lt Col D.S. Wooles MBE
157 Lt Col G.D. Lilley
158 Lt Col G.B.L. Fox

159 Col Brian Colston
160 Central London Branch RASC/ RCT Association
161 Sidney John Cottrell
162 Lt Col P. Firth
163 SSgt "Taff" John
164 Maj J.McD. Ferrier
165 Lt Col (Retd) H.R. Twitchet
166 Reg Judge
167 Brig J. Heptinstall
168 Capt L. Murray McCullough
169 Cpl F.F.A. Nunez
170 Brig D.T. Kinnear OBE
171 F. Cross, RASC/RCT Assn
172 Maj (QM) C.J. Mears
173 Capt B.L. Tarr
174 Col R.L. Wallis
175 Lt Col N.A. Smith MBE, TD
176 Brian F. Little Ex-RASC
177 Lt Col B.B. Bateson
178 Col J.D. Payne
179 Maj P.T. McGrath RASC RCT RLC
180 S.W.R. Kent Ex-RASC
181 Maj A.B. Drewe
182 WO1 J.E. Reynolds RASC/RCT 1946-68
183 Lt Col Nigel Plowright
184 Lt Col (Retd) S. Husband
185 Maj F.S.C. Hancock (Retd)
186 Maj A.S. Taylor RCT
187 Maj R.C. Croslegh
188 Col C.G.K. Underhill 1951-85
189 MSSgt W.H.J. Jenkins RASC Jersey Boy
190 A. Baguley
191 Maj A.J.G. Chambers
192 Maj R.A. Mathie
193 WO2 (CSM) R. Shepherd RASC
194 Lt Col J.R. Sherburn MBE
195 Lt Col R. Vaughan-Stanley
196 J.W. Reid Ex-RASC
197 Capt H.V. Lewis MBE
198 Brig D.W.E. Hancox
199 Lt Col Peter Robinson MA, RCT
200 Cpl E. Sunley RASC
201 SSgt Thomas J. Addley (Ex-Jersey Boy)
202 Lt Col J.B. Lee
203 WO1 J.S.S. C Chalmers MISM RCT
204 Capt Mark Shephard Adjt GTR
205 (Ex-WO1) H.W. Stephenson BEM
206 Maj R.C.A. McAllister
207 Maj C.W.P. Coan
208 H. Egerton
209 Maj C.D.M. Harris
210 Lt Col D.W. Brown RCT
211 Lt C.A. Moores MILDM RCT
212 A.J. Ferrier
213 Maj F.R. Corner
214 Brig D.J. Sutton OBE
215 Maj Gen A. L. Meier OBE
216 J.A. Needs
217 SSgt C.R.E. Mitchell
218 L.P. Hall RCT
219 Jolly Joff, 27
220 F.G. Willetts TD
221 Lt Col P.W. Morling OBE
222 Capt M.F. White
223 Maj E. (Spike) Hughes

224 Cpl T.E. Bell
225 Brig J.B. Sandberg CBE
226 Maj A.J. Hurst RCT (V)
227 Cpl R.B. Stone
228 Maj D.J. Norton
229 Flt Lt M.J. Dunn RAuxAF
230 Dr R.R.L. Thomas DBA, PhD, FCIT
231 Capt J. R. McGuidan RCT BA(Hons)
232 Lt Col P.S. Reehal
233 Robert Geering
234 21(NI) Tpt & Mov Regt RCT
235 Lt Col Leslie Huxtable
236 Maj M.J. Sheen TD
237 Brig R.G. Harmer
238 Col C.J. Constable
239 Maj A.J. Wood
240 68 Sqn RCT
241 Sgt J.C. Anderson
242 Capt A.D.H. Lapidus
243 Lt Col J.W. Heath TD
244 Sgt B.D.G. Bradley
245 Brig G.D. Williams
246 Maj D.G. Balcombe
247 Lt T.J. Burchett-Vass
248 K.C. Moore
249 Maj G.C. Walmsley RASC
250 Capt D.B. Halliday
251 Maj A.F. Wiliamson RCT
252 Lt Col A.J.M. Smetham RCT
253 Maj P.B. Hadden
254 Maj Gen Peter Benson CBE
255 Capt G.V. Wright
256 Maj S.B. Doudney
257 K.R. Chapman RASC
258 Lt Col R.W. Armstrong
259 Maj Gen J.R. Reynolds
260 Capt A.B. McLeod RCT
261 Lt Col G.J. Shawley TD
262 WO2 T. McIntosh BEM
263 John Crombie RASC
264 Lt Col V.H. Band MC
265 Col M.C. McHenry, US Army Attaché, London
266 Maj P.E. Alberry RCT
267 G.M. Chantler
268 J.C. Holliman
269 Lt Col S.J. Barr
270 WO1 M. Ward
271 Col G.W. Somerville
272 Brig M.W. Betts CBE, ADC
273 Maj I.H. Stewart RCT
274 Col A.E.W. Stormer
275 Cpl L. Jones RASC
276 Lt Col John Walters
277 Sgt A.G. Crowson RASC
278 Lt Col R.M. Wilkinson TD
279 Capt W.H. Goddard MBE
280 Lt Col W.G. Osmond
281 Lt Col B. Morris
282 Maj I.W. MacArthur
283 Lt Col C.R.C. Green
284 Lt Col F.C. Matthews
285 Maj (QM) L.R. Dolan
286 WO2 (RQMS) Reynolds
287 Maj (QM) D.J. Winkle
288 Lt Col B.C. Neeves RCT

289 Capt J.H. Gutteridge RASC Jersey Boy
290 Maj (QM) R.H. Allen RCT
291 Army Museum Ogilby Trust
292 Lt Col D.A. Mead TD RCT (V)
293 David J. Tran
294 Lt Col A.R. Allum
295 Maj R.M. Aickin TD
296 Capt P.J. Beauchamp
297 Lt Col (Retd) J.A. Lee
298 Lt Col R.P.M. Rendall MBE, RCT
299 Maj M C S. Alexander RCT
300 SSgt B. Bridgeman RCT
301 Col M.C. Sims
302 Brig M.J. Squire OBE
303 Capt (Retd) H.N.F. MacDonnell
304 Maj I.S. Ormerod
305 Maj J.E. Thomas TD
306 Lt Col G.M.J. Grieve RCT
307 Capt D.A. Kelly
308 Capt A.I. Griffiths
309 Lt Col J.D. Fielden MBE, RCT
310 Maj D.J. Le Cheminant
311 Lt Col K.M. Tutt OBE, RCT
312 Dvr L.G. Luckhurst
313 Maj C.J. Upchurch RCT
314 Ex-Sgt N.I. Whitford RASC
315 SSgt S.J. Melinn RCT
316 Maj J.M. Hay RCT
317 WO2 (SSM) M. Thornley
318 Maj N.P. Humpherson RCT
319 Lt Col A.J.C. Fisher MBE
320 Capt R.A. Gibson RCT
321 Maj M.R.P. James RCT
322 Maj J.A. Clover RCT
323 Tony Jackson
324 WO2 (SSM) P. Thomas
325 Lt Col D.J.C. Wickes
326 Lt Col (Retd) C.A. Murray
327 Maj T.H. Murray
328 Maj A.J. Shipley
329 Bath Branch, RASC/RCT Assoc
330 Maj Gordon T. Hamilton USA TC
331 Capt P.A. Marshall
332 WO2 Roy Scholey
333 Maj J.H. Innes TD
334 Maj Joff Williams
335 76 Sqn RCT
336 SSgt I. Cameron 21 Sqn 3 ADTR RCT
337
339 Depôt & Trg Regt RCT
340 Capt J.J. Brown
341 SO3 G1 HQ 33 Armd Bde
342 SSgt C. Joinson
343 Capt (QM) T.A.G. McEwen RCT (V)
344 Ex-SSgt M.A. Bradford RASC/RCT
345 C.S. Beadmore
346 Lt Col M.A. Willson-Lloyd
347 Capt B.S. Bartlett
348 Maj A. Beveridge
349 Brig D.N. Locke OBE
350 Lt A.P. Hoff
351 WO2(RQMS) Pete Collins 4 ADTR RCT
352 Derrick Cooke
353 Maj A.J. Mutch RCT
354 S Sgt J. Anderson
355 SSupt H. Foertsch 636 MCTG

356 Maj L.R. Tucker RCT
357 Capt M.A. Jordan
358 John Colley
359 Hugh Manuel
360 R.E. Thomas
361 Capt M. Howard RCT
362 Edward H. Thorpe
363 Lt Col R.W. Armstrong
364 Maj P. Whyte
365 Maj Andrew D.G. Teitge RCT
366 F.G. O'Connell
367 Lt Col B.H.R. Coles
368 WO2 (SSM) R. E. Murphy
369 Lt Col. M.H. Charteris-Black
370 Maj D.I. Hollas RCT
371 Maj T.E.D. Searles
372 Maj N.T. Start (OC 33 Sqn RCT)
373 Lt Col D.S. Barker-Simson
374 Maj Frank Hall
375 P.R.L. Lee-Emery
376 Lt Col D.A.G. Welsford
377 Maj P.M. Smith RCT
378 Col T.M. Macartney
379 Lt Col I.G. Thomas
380 WO1 Mark J. Bremner RCT
381 Lt Col (Retd) M.J.S. Applegate
382 Capt Neil Cowan
383-
386 237 Sqn RCT (V) Midlands
387 Capt A.J. Gale
388 Edwin Horlington
389 WO1 (RSM) G.E. Allen
390 SSgt R. Penney
391 John H. Andrew
392 Norman King
393 Lt Col D.N. Wright MBE
394 Maj R.A. Griffiths
395 Maj P.J. McGuigan
396 Capt S.J. Mackenzie RCT
397 Capt H. Jones RCT
398 WO2 A Bowring
399 Maj S.P. Cowlam RCT
400 Charles W. Turner (Ex-Sgt RASC)
401 Maj (Retd) R.E. Kershaw
402 WO2 D.H. Rice
403 F.J. Moore
404 Sgt D. Tasker
405 Maj (Retd) K.W. Blease
406 John Herbert
407 WO2 C.R. Woodley RCT
408 24 Tpt & Mov Regt RCT
409 Joe Jensen - Singapore
410 Maj M.D. Vickers RCT
411 Col D.H. St C. Collins MBE, TD
412 P.G. Cole
413 219 (West Riding) Sqn RCT (V)
414   WO & Sgts Mess
415 Maj G. Henderson MBE, RCT
416 WO1 (SSM) J.A.K. Smith MSM
417 Lt Col Grattan Hart (1939-1965)
418 Dvr L. Wilson RASC
419 Maj W.M. Carlisle RCT
420 Maj M.F. Barlow 56 Sqn RCT
421 WO & Sgts Mess 10 Regt RCT
422 Maj R.B. Hobson MBE
423 Lt Col R.F. Grevatte-Ball

424 WO & Sgts Mess RCT, London Dist
425 Lt Col J.H. Hitch
426 7 Sqn RCT, Officers & Men Past & Pres.
427 Maj J.A. Gibson
428 157 Tpt Regt RCT (V)
429 WO2 (SSM) S.M. Cooper
430 230 Sqn RCT (V)
431 Defence Office, Swiss Embassy
432 Reginald Minion
433 Maj P.G. Coates ERD
434 Maj H. Britton Johnson
435 Col C.W. Wilson
436 WO2 A P. Lambert RCT
437 Maj W.E. Campbell CD (Late RCASC)
438 M.R. Mealyer
439 A.C. Baker
440 Const J. Brodie
441 Const C. Haralambeas
442 SSgt W McNiven
443 David Cann
444 Maj D.P. Roberts RCT
445 Officers' Mess, 152 (Ulster)
         Ambulance Regt RCT (V)
446 WO2 Bloomfield 23 Para Fd Amb
447 J.I. Colligan BEM
448 47 AD Sqn RCT
449 Lt Col E.J. Hunter RCT
450 Capt D.T.L. Boshier RASC,
         RCT, RLC
451 Maj (QM) F.J. Selleck
452 Maj N.E.O. Notley MBE, TD, RCT (V)
453 Capt Mark (Sparky) Corthine BEM, RCT
454 Maj S.R. Roberts
455 221 Squadron RCT (V)
456 Maj W.M. Young TD, RCT (V)
457 Maj A.J. Neal RCT 1979-93
458 Andrew B. Chisholm
459 41 Squadron RCT
460 D.A. Irvine
461 Sgt N. Storm
462 Lt Col J.M. May RCT
463 Maj A.L. Jones RCT
464 WO2 Heaney
465 SSgt Jolly
466 Cpl Newman
467 Cpl Hughes
468 Dvr McMahan
469 Dvr Perry
470 Dvr Phillips
471 Capt P. Foley RCT
472 Maj M.C. Cafe TD, JP, RCT (V)
473 Lt Col S.A.G. Simms MBE
474 SSgt S.E. Rogers
475 Cpl D.M. Allen
476 Sgt N. Land
477 Stephen Robert Turrell
478 H.E. Hudgell
479 WO2 (SSM) P. Griffiths RCT
480 Capt P.J. Shields QGM, RCT
481 Sydney J. Caddell
482 Lt Col J.M. Bowles MBE, RCT
483 238 Sqn RCT (V)
484 Maj P.J. Clayton RCT
485
486 G.J. Pugh
487 A. Yeldham

488 Victor Cook
489 Laurie Manton
490 Alan J. Kelly
491 G. Curphey
492 W.H. Goddard MBE
493 Capt (Retd) R. Minns
494 Reginald William Wood
495 Gordon G. Boulton
496 P.E. Bradick
497 Maj (Retd) V.R. Boulton
498 WO1 (RSM) B.C. Young RCT
499 R. Guest MBE
500 Wimbridge Haulage
501 W. Roger
502 SSupt W. Kophler 605 MCTG
503 K. Emmerson
504 21 (NI) Tpt & Mov Regt RCT
505 Andrew Elgeti
506 Lt Col A.S.A. Carr
507 Roy V. Hatherley
508 Maj M. J. Culnane MBE
509 Capt M.A. Bendall RCT
510 William Bessell
511 Sgt P. Harding
512 Maj (Retd) A. Harding
513 L.D. Evans
514 Bernard Kerry
515 Maj A.B. Anderson MBE
516 Capt John R. Tomkins
517 SSgt I. J. Mitchell BEM
518 Lt Col S.T.M. Pledger
519 R.A. Craig
520 Lt Col J.P. Shoesmith TD
521 WO2 M.A. Bennett BEM
522 Sgt J.P. Harrowell
523 Hugh MacGregor Mackintosh
524 WO2 R.V. Pearce
525 Maj (Retd) M.A. Patton
526 Col P.W.H. Jay
527 Frederick P.R. Ward
528 David Preece
529 Keith Frood
530 Brig T.A.K. Savage MBE
531 Cpl A.R. Williams RSI
532 SSgt S.P. Weller
533 H.G. Miles
534 Maj K.A. Hearson
535 Ian W. Fawkner
536 P.S. Norcott
538 Lt Col G.C.E. Crew OBE
538 Col A.G. Bell
539 Capt R.M. Pratt RCT
540 S.L.L. Eggleton
541 Philip Baker
542 Lt Col John E.C. Lewis
543 Roy Clark (WO1 RSM)
544 Capt (Retd) G.F. Charlton
545 A.M. Carbin
546 14 Squadron RCT
547 Alistair J. Deas
548 H.M. Le Feuvre
549 Maj A.J. Pashby TD
550 Capt (Retd) G.G.H. Snelgar
551 K.F. Morris
552 Maj (Retd) F.M. Nuttall
553 Capt W. Tate

158

554 Capt K. Whiteley RCT
555 Capt I.G. Ratazzi
556 SSgt D.M. Rowlands
557 Maj P.J.C. Payne
558 RASC, RCT Derby Branch
559 Col W.H. Slack ERD DC
560 Graven Hill Sergeants' Mess
561 Maj J. H. Forrest
562 WO2 (SSM) D.F. Harvey
563 D.C. Donald
564 Raymond Hoare
565 Bernard Williams
566 Simon F. Jenkins
567 C.P. Baillie
568 Col Leslie Smith
569 D.M. Flynn
570 Royal Hospital, Chelsea
571 N.C. King
572 Maj (Retd) L.H. Oldham RASC
573 Lt Col. P.E. Burton
574 Capt D.H.R. MacDonald
575 A.E. Arnold
576 K.C. Moore
577 Lt Col R.W.E. House
578 Eric Franklin RASC 1943-54
579 Maj C. Strong RCT
580 Lt Col W.R. Bloxwich
581 John Pendlebury
582 Maj J.D. Ball RCT
583 Maj R.M. Devonshire RCT
584 WO2 C.H.J. Holdsworth
585 B.T.C Smith
586 Oberst Klaus Hammel
587 G.H. Boorman
588 Peter Buchanan
589 SSgt Ronald Tarn
590 Lt Col A.R.M. Adams MBE
591 Paul Benton
592 T.J. Slater
593 Sgt A.T. Lowe
594 Col R.N. Harris
595 Capt M.F. White
596 George W. Hook
597 Lt Col Terry Lees
598 Peter Hooker
599 D. Rawlingson Plant
600 Brig (Retd) M. H. Turner
601 Officers' Mess 153 Arty Sp
    Regt RCT (V)
602 Sergeants' Mess 153 Arty Sp Regt RCT (V)
603 SSgt R.R. Shepherd
604 F.C. Butcher
605 Ian Masterton
606 M.J. McMahon
607 SSgt B.L. Long
608 Capt Byron Thomas Lewis
609 Lt Col S.J. Searle MBE, RCT
610 SSgt J.R. Rowe
611
612 T. Ward
613 Maj S.M. Loasby
614 Brig J.C. O'Connor
615 Maj J.E. Tong
616 Lady Travers
617 SSgt M. Hensman
618 Maj J.R. Boulton

619 Col W.P. Howells
620 Garry Frith
621 Reg Hamblen
622 Lt Col T.E. Nelson OBE
623 Col (Retd) Dennis Charles Wildish
624 Allan J. Maddern
625 F.E. Hammond
626 Maj G.M. Roberts RASC, RCT 1958-77
627 Stephen S. Haywood
628 WO2 T.W. Pointon
629 Lt Col (R) J.F. Waterfield
630 SQMS D. Greenwood Ex-RASC
631 Maj M.I. McKinnon RCT
632 C.J. Simon
633 David Downham
634 Maj W.J. Norman RCT/V
635 John Gillard Watson
636 Maj (Retd) M.E. Thorp
637 Maj R.H.G. Barton
638 Capt R.L. Forbes-Ritte
639 Maj D.W. Dawson
640 Sgt C.A. Fisher
641 Maj I.A. MacEachen
642 Maj T.W. Gough MBE, TD
643 H.R. Hoffman TD
644 Lt Col C.N. Thompson
645 R.J. Roweth
646 A.H. Jones
647-
648 K.M. Pemberthy
649 Maj Barry Hadlow
650 T.H. Ridgway
651 B.A. Joyce
652 Maj C.A. (Tony) Priestley
653 Michael David Anstee
654 Col D.W. Rogers
655 J.E.L. Christmas
656 Thomas Kerr
657 William Astin
658 Henry Browse
659 D.J. Wride
660 WO2 Eric Broom
661 Jim Carty
662 Leslie Cooper
663 Lt Col A.L. Bridger OBE, RCT
664 Maj B.V. Wynn-Wernick
665 L.J. Walker
666 D. Ferbrache
667 Col (Retd) R.A. Crawley OBE
668 F.H. Crowhurst
669 Kenneth James Kirkpatrick
670 J.A. Shield
671 Maj K.H. Crockford MC
672 Sgt J.D. Fordham
673 M.J. Melaugh
674 A.R.M. Forbes
675 Lt Col (Retd) H.L. Dalwood
676 Col W.H. Slack
677 D.A. Sellers BEM
678 E.S. Lewis
679 I.M. Brewer
680 W. McKernan
681 R.W.E. House
682 B.W. Billingham
683 Col D.L. Davies TD
684 SSgt I. Cameron

685 Col D.F. Easten MC
686 Maj T.E. Owens
687 Capt G. Hill RCT
688 J.H. Wyss MBE
689 Robert Hughes
690 Capt (Retd) N. Coulson
691 WO1 D.V. Hill RCT (V)
692 W.R. Thompson
693 Col Philip C. Medenbach
694 Maj Paul R. Sheridan TD
695 Maj J.Y. McCallum
696 Jack Cheatle
697 D.I. Weir
698 Lt Col D.J. Jackson
699 Maj R.N. Owsley
700 Maj J.R. Brinley TD
701 S. Binney BEM
702 W.R.A. Selbie
703 Cpl Alan Wing
704 Ex-Cpl P.G. Basey W/S RASC
705 Col A.R. Tapp
706 Maj L.R. Bedborough
707-
708 17 P & M Regt RCT (PRI)
709 Derek Heffron
710 Capt M.J. Hassall
711 Maj P.G. May RCT
712 Arthur Scott Thompson
713 Maj D. Durham
714 Ian Weekley
715 Capt D.N. Ashcroft
716 Maj C.H. Maginniss
717 David Rees
718 Lt Col A.R. Skipper
719 Lt Col. J.A. Bartlet (Retd)
720 K. Laws
721 P.E. Fisher
722 Lt Col (Retd) J.H.B. Molyneux
723 Lt S.A. Summersgill
724 Chartered Institute of Transport
725 WO2 (SSM) Barsby
726 Wilson Clydesdale
727 WO1 T.D.N. Wilcox RCT
728 Maj A. Bentley
729 Maj T.C. Byrne
730 Lt Col M.J. Rust RCT
731 V.E. Mahan
732 Lt Col Wm. C. Munro OBE, TD
733 James A.M. Smith
734 Ex-T/56945 CSM R.L. Jones
735 E.H. Reeder
736 Capt A.G. Fortey
737 A.G. Jackson
738 WO1 (RSM) P.B. Widdows
739 M.F.I. Cubitt
740 Maj G.D. Kneale MBE
741 Capt T.M. Coppin RCT
742 L.S. Edwards
743 Maj K.C. Hobbs RCT
744 Maj E.F. Palmer MBE, RCT
745 M.S. Robertshawe
746 Lt Col B.C. Vaughan
747 Lt Col H.P. Higgins
748 Lt Col H.M.M. Deighton
749 Wg Cdr C.F. Hoare
750 Major A.W. Fisher

751 Mrs Janet Martin
752 Mrs Thora Myatt
753 Col Arnold Lewis
754 Sgt Reginald Thomas Cranton
755 E.K. Williams
756 Fred Davis
757 Col I.J. Hellberg OBE
758 Lt Col A.S. Parker
759 Fred Cason
760 Maj P. O'Sullivan
761 W. Lenc
762 H. Kubinski MSM
763 Ronald Wood
764 WO1 (RSM) R.L.D. Booles
765 Sgt P.K. Green
766 Sgt D. Williams
767 SSgt S.D. Rees
768 Capt K.M. Davidson TD
769 Capt A. Ryan
770 Col John Baxter CBE, TD
771 H.G. Graham-Battersby
772 Sgt John Ball
773 Lt Col (Retd) P.W.M. Roberts
774 Maj K.B. Wilson
775 Brig W.M.E. White
776 Capt D.J. Lafferty MBE, JP
777 Sydney Balgarnie
778 The Revd A.M. Bartlett
779 Col M.J. Blyth
780 Central Library RMAS
781 Maj P.R. Stabb TD RCT (V)
782
783 F.M. Stewart
784 Maj C.H. Sealey
785 Maj V.J. Sanders
786 Capt (Retd) P.D. Morris
787 Maj V.E.W. Surridge
788 Ian Munro
789 M. Rushton
790 P.K. Orris
791 SSgt R. Fishwick RCT
792 Maj S. Graham RCT
793 SSgt Alan Mortimer
794-
795 Capt K. Dunstan
796 Capt S.D. Glynn
797 WO2 (SSM) T. Raven RCT
798 Maj D.I. Snowden RCT
799 John Silbermann OBE, FCIT, FRSA
800 Capt D.R. Dugan RCT
801 Capt C. Vooght
802 A. Hilton
803 Maj (Retd) P.W. Myatt
804 G.B. Palmer JP
805 Jack G. Scott
806 Allan Foreman
807 P.B.G. Cummings
808 Brian Loftus
809 G.P. Walsh
810 Capt T. Harrison MBE, CStJ, TD
811 P.J. Doyle
812 K. Bailes
813 Maj C.J. Barkes MSc, RCT
814 Sgt Michael Kelly

815 SSgt Stuart Owens
816 WO2 T.M. Scates
817 Maj R.S. Card
818 Sgt S.J. Wardle RCT
819 SSgt Roskelly
820 Maj The Revd Graham Thorne
821 Lt S.P.J. Hood RCT
822 T.L. José JP
823 Lt Col R.H. Hatton
824 L.M. Evanson-Goddard
825
826 Col Harold Smith OBE, JP, DL
827 T.B. Llewellyn
828 Major (QM) E.A. Ford
829 Stanley J. Little
830 George Francis Collie
831 Maj J.R. Nelson RCT
832 D.J.G. Mellor
833 Keith Affleck
834 Lt Col D.R. Black
835 M.E.G. Taylor
836 L.D. Evans
837 W.J. Diment
838 Vaughan H. Baker
839 J.M.B. Gotch
840 SSgt J.T. West RCT
841 J.E. Middleditch
842 Lt Col M.A. Ponikowski RCT
843 G.G. Hardaker
844 Lt Col J.R. Wallace MBE
845 John Emms
846 P.R. King
847 David Wayman
848 J. McGill
849 A.H. Allerston
850 Capt C. Phillips RCT
851 C.H. Moss
852 J. Clementson
853
854 Maj P.T. McGrath RASC, RCT, RLC
855 WO1 D.L. Morton
856 WO2 B.J. Keate RCT
857 R.S. Rowland
858 Brig A.K. Dixon
859 Montgomeryshire Branch, RASC/RCT Assoc
860 Lt Col M.J. Paine RCT
861 C.A. Hart
862 Capt P.A. Corney RCT (V)
863 Lt Col C.J. Doland
864 Maj M.E. Thorpe
865 Brig A.J. Simmons
866
867 Mr & Mrs C.P. Dixon-Warren
868
869 16 Tank Transporter Squadron RCT
870 C. Whant
871 D.A. Broomfield Ex-Sgt
872 Bruce Watson
873 WO2 T.L. Gray
874 Lt Col S. Hubbard OBE
875 Lucy M. Barron (Capt)
876 Denis E. Davidge
877 Clifford Wilson

878 Maj A.G. Parker RCT
879 Lt Mark John
880 R. Boyeldieu
881 David Sandles
882 Teesside Branch, RASC/RCT Assoc
883 Lee Brady
884 Lt Col P.M. Carolan RCT
885 WO2 (SQMS) M. Brown RCT
886 Lt Col H.E. Brewis
887 G.J. Yeoman
888 Capt C.C. Powell
889 H.L. Wheeler
890 I.R. Mosedale
891 Lt Col S.S.N. Grundy
892 S.G. Steele
893 R.N. Howard
894 A. Leslie Palmer
895 T.J. Gilbert
896 Colchester Branch RASC/RCT Assn
897 D.W. Parkin (WO)
898 Lt Col Ivor Renwick OBE
899 Maj M.G. Wilkes
900 A.F. Dorling
901 Maj R.G. Beavis MBE RCT
902
903 Cpl N. Magee
904 Lt D.A. Farleigh
905 Nicholas Baker
906 Victor Roberts
907 Col Colin Mearns OBE, TD
908 D.A. Goodchild
909 Maj H.K. Trundell TD
910 Maj (Retd) E.R.L. Wade
911 Mrs F.P. Carroll
912 Maj Gen Sir John Potter KBE, CB
913 Robert Hughes
914 Wilfred Sherratt
915 Capt A.C. Law RCT
916 Mrs M. Lucas
917 W.J. Heaps
918 Brighton, Hove & District RASC/RCT Association
919 J.F.M. Scruton
920 T. Howard
921 L. S. Keelty
922 Maj Charles Wilson
923 John Brodie
924 A.P. Fashey
925 Maj D.J.R. Martin RCT
926 Mr & Mrs V.J. Bowles
927 Col C.K. Gillman-Wells
928 Lt Col C.M. Steirn
929 WO2 (SQMS) P.R. Lawton
930 Capt F.R. White RCT
931 WO1 G.P. Tilley
932 Col A.S. Feldman
933 J.H.W. Beardwell
934 Lt Col J.B. Massey
935 James Kerry (Ex-Cpl RCT)
936 N.I. Wightman
937
986 The Royal Corps of Transport

Remaining Names Unlisted